Ethics in the Practice of Law
A Seven Springs Center Project

Ethics in the Practice of Law

Geoffrey C. Hazard, Jr.

New Haven and London   Yale University Press
1978

Published with assistance from the foundation established in memory of Philip Hamilton McMillan of the Class of 1894, Yale College.

Copyright © 1978 by Seven Springs Farm Center, Inc. All rights reserved. This book may not be reproduced, in whole or in part, in any form (beyond that copying permitted by Sections 107 and 108 of the U. S. Copyright Law and except by reviewers for the public press), without written permission from the publishers.

Designed by Thos. Whitridge and set in IBM Baskerville type. Printed in the United States of America by The Vail-Ballou Press, Binghamton, N. Y.

Published in Great Britain, Europe, Africa, and Asia (except Japan) by Yale University Press, Ltd., London. Distributed in Australia and New Zealand by Book & Film Services, Artarmon, N.S.W., Australia; and in Japan by Harper & Row, Publishers, Tokyo Office.

Library of Congress Cataloging in Publication Data

Hazard, Geoffrey C., Jr.
  Ethics in the practice of law.

  Report of a symposium held in 1976 at Seven Springs Center.
  Includes index.
  1. Legal ethics—United States. I. Seven Springs Center. II. Title.
KF306.H3   1978   174'.3   77-16357
ISBN 0-300-02206-9

To my son Jim

Contents

Foreword	ix
Introduction	xi
1. An Ethical Lawyer	1
2. The Official Rules	15
3. Who Is the Client?	43
4. Lawyer for the Situation	58
5. Conflict of Interest	69
6. Unpopular Clients	87
7. Fees	97
8. The Revolving Door	107
9. The Adversary System	120
10. Advise and Dissent	136
11. Concluding Reflections	150
Appendix	154
Index	156

Foreword

Seven Springs Center was established by Yale University in 1973, pursuant to a bequest by the late Mrs. Eugene Meyer, Jr. In keeping with her intention and Yale's purpose, the Center's aim is to promote scholarship, creativity, and understanding in matters of major intellectual, cultural, and public significance. To this end it sponsors symposia that bring together persons in academia, the professions, business, and government to seek mutual enlightenment and to stimulate dialogue about where America is on particular issues, where we are heading and why, and what the processes and priorities should be.

One range of subjects prominent on the Seven Springs agenda is the ethics of the practitioners of professions central to the functioning of the American society: lawyers, physicians, bureaucrats, elected and appointed representatives of the populace.

The Center was fortunate to enlist Geoffrey C. Hazard, Jr., of the Yale Law School, to plan an agenda for a two-part symposium on the ethical lawyer—the Center's first and thus pilot project under the rubric of ethical practice. We were also fortunate that Oscar M. Ruebhausen, an eminent attorney in New York City, agreed to chair the discussions. In that role he helped shape the agenda and select the participants in the sessions held in the summer of 1976 and presided over these with great perception and wisdom.

There were twenty-five participants in the discussion, all of them members of the country's professional elite and most of them lawyers. The lawyers included partners of large prestigious law firms located in major cities, general counsel of large corporations, the chief counsel of a large legal aid agency, a federal judge, the director of a foundation concerned with law and the legal profession, lawyers of similar rank in the government, and professors of law at nationally recognized universities. The nonlawyers included a sociologist and two political scientists, each also associated with a leading university, and persons with long experience and impressive achievement in government and business. A list of the members of the symposium is appended to this book.

It is a rule at Seven Springs, designed to encourage participants to speak freely and candidly, that they are never quoted. At the same time, the light, even the heat, generated by the private discussion can be—must be—shared with a wider constituency. Professor Hazard has fashioned a report on the subject that draws expertly on the symposium, on previously published papers available to its members, and on his own very considerable knowledge. Seven Springs expresses its gratitude to him for a significant contribution to understanding of a range of issues too often dimly perceived and inadequately confronted.

Seven Springs Center is administratively and financially separate from Yale; its costs are met in part from an endowment bequeathed by Mrs. Meyer, along with Seven Springs Farm. The costs of symposia and other events are funded separately by contributions from corporations, foundations, and individuals. The Center gratefully acknowledges the support of this project received from the Ford Foundation and the Council for Legal Education for Professional Responsibility.

                                        Joseph N. Green, Jr.
                                        President, Seven Springs Center

Mount Kisco
August 1977

Introduction

The behavior of large corporations and top echelons of government is a grave public concern, and was so before Watergate. That behavior is judged properly, though not exclusively, by whether it conforms to the law's requirements. How these organizations adapt their behavior to the requirements of the law is determined in part by the substance and style of the legal advice they get, and that in turn is determined in part by what their legal advisers conceive their professional role and responsibilities to be.

The problem has many forms. Why, apparently, did none of the Nixon lawyers think it was his business that the plumbers were. using illegal methods? Why did the legal department of Gulf not raise questions about that company's political contributions? Why did a Wall Street partner let a stock issue be sold that he knew was shadowy and maybe shady? There is a simple answer to these questions: Power and money are involved, and lawyers can be bought. But this answer, servicable as it has been, proves too much. The decision makers in all organizations are concerned with power and money and not all lawyers will hire out to do whatever a client might want. There must be differences here, as there are among loan companies, auto dealers, and zoning boards, and the lawyers who represent them. The differences in the end perhaps are ones of character, an old-fashioned term that means everything and nothing. But character, in life as in art, is revealed as a response to practical dilemmas. To appraise character requires appreciating what those dilemmas are, and such is the aim of this study.

The question at hand should be seen in proper perspective.

Corporations and government agencies are not the instruments of their legal counsel. The behavior of large organizations has many other determinants, most of them much more influential than legal advice. Among these determinants are the understood aims of the organization (Is a corporation supposed to accomplish more than making a maximum return on its stockholders' investment? What, exactly, are the objectives of a government regulatory agency?); the economic and political incentives and restrictions that shape the organization's alternatives at any given point (profit, political survival, long-range effectiveness, social respectability, for example); and the ambitions and inhibitions of its leaders, staff, constituents, and critics. But these determinants all have significant legal components, such as the antitrust laws, the election contribution laws, the policies of regulatory agencies, the powers of Congress, etc. In more general terms, legal controls on large organizations operate within an economic and political milieu that is defined in important respects by "the law" at large. What the lawyers for these organizations think "the law" is and how they perform their function in its application therefore are considerations of some consequence for organizational behavior. Moreover, large organizations, much more than small ones or private individuals, are attuned to a constant flow of legal advice before and during their critical decision making, rather than obtaining legal assistance only after the fact and in the face of external legal sanctions. In most transactions of a large organization, the pronouncements of its legal advisors will be its chief source of legal guidance.

In absolute numbers, relatively few lawyers are engaged in the kind of practice with which this book is principally concerned. Somewhat over 400,000 persons are presently authorized to practice law in this country and probably something like 300,000 make their living as practitioners of some kind. Of this number probably no more than 10

INTRODUCTION xiii

percent are regularly involved in providing legal services that directly and significantly impinge on the activities of large corporations and major government agencies. But this group's concept of its ethical responsibilities is of consequence far out of proportion to its size. It includes a large fraction of the practitioners who are best versed in technical legal knowledge, most proficient in professional art, most highly compensated, and most often occupants of positions of authority, prestige, and influence within the profession.[1] In this sense they are the models of legal counsel in the modern industrial system. Furthermore, and a point to be developed as this account proceeds, the ethical problems of this professional group exemplify problems that are encountered, sometimes more vividly and sometimes less so, by all lawyers in the practice of their profession.

The ethics of lawyers in general, and those serving powerful clients in particular, have always been the subject of popular anxiety and suspicion. Public esteem for the legal profession has been ambivalent, in that while law and administered justice express fundamental moral values in our form of government, lawyers are often thought of as dissimulators who pervert justice. The practicing bar has learned to live with this hostility in its milder forms, satisfied that on the whole it has adequately performed essential social functions. Of late, however, there seems to have been a qualitative change in this situation. The public attitude is more deeply distrustful and the profession itself has ceased to be secure in the conviction that its vocation is indeed a learned art performed in the spirit of public service. It is going through a crisis of public confidence and self-confidence.

In broader terms, the problem is one aspect of the wide-

---

1. See Laumann and Heinz, "Specialization and Prestige in the Legal Profession: The Structure of Deference," 1977 *Am. Bar Found. Research J.* 155.

spread present distrust of our institutions. This attitude has developed by cumulative process over the past decade or so and has become pervasive and entrenched. It attaches not only to public office as such but to the "power structure" generally, that is, to all who hold positions of special power, authority, or duty. The legal profession conspicuously is within this suspect class. In the public sector, many officials, permanent and temporary, are members of the legal profession. In the private sector—business corporations, charitable institutions, voluntary associations such as unions and trade groups—lawyers give legal form to the very organization of the system and are almost always involved in decisions at moments of crisis or serious conflict.

In still broader perspective, many ethical dilemmas of the legal profession exemplify those confronting occupational elites generally, including doctors, accountants, journalists, politicians, and business executives.[2] The weight of public responsibility falling on these elites has become heavier in proportion as the task of defining and resolving issues of community interest and welfare has increasingly devolved upon professional specialists. More and more in the affairs of modern life, the professional specialist is the only one who really knows the intricacies of the situation, if only in the limited framework of his professional role. At the same time, the decisions he makes and the positions he takes are more visible, partly because he no longer works alone but in collaboration with colleagues, paraprofessionals, and professionals in adjacent fields. Professionals generally, and lawyers among them, thus must now perform more demanding tasks

---

2. See, e.g., "The Troubled Professions," *Business Week*, August 16, 1976. For an exploration of some of the ethical problems of some of the professions, see Hodges, ed., *Social Responsibility and the Professions,* vols. I (1975) and II (1976).

INTRODUCTION xv

without the protective mystique that formerly made them accountable only unto themselves. The modern professional also seems more vulnerable than his predecessor. A century ago, the professional usually was or became a member of the propertied class, with attendant economic, political, and social status and autonomy. Today he is usually a self-made person in the literal sense that he has become what he is through training and professional standing. In this respect, he is like his counterparts in large business enterprise, where the managerial group consists mostly of successful employees rather than owner-entrepreneurs, or in government, where the elected group consists mostly of successful publicists. His economic situation is dependent on a present income stream and that in turn is dependent on his maintaining position in his profession. Correlatively, if his professional position is impaired by ethically questionable conduct, disastrous effects can ensue not only for his practice but for his family, his social status, and his self-esteem.

Moreover, the work setting of the modern professional has undergone a profound change, arising from the fact, earlier alluded to, that he works in groups. From an ethical viewpoint, this circumstance has at least three implications. First, he is subject not only to the norms affirmed by his profession at large but also, for better or worse, to the "shop norms" of his firm, agency, or department. Second, he is subject to strong inhibitions, on the ground of "team play," against questioning the conduct of other professionals of equal or superior rank with whom he interacts in his work. And third, how he resolves the ethical problems he confronts is more readily visible to others. Traditionally, the idealized professional is a soloist, technically and ethically sufficient unto himself and personally accountable as such. In modern fact, he has less personal control in resolving ethical dilemmas arising in his work, but also vicarious responsibility for decisions made by coprofessionals. Perhaps it is this conjunction of reduced autonomy and enlarged responsibility that explains much of his present ethical distress.

There is no dearth of commentary on corporation lawyers' ethics. Most of it can be characterized as polemical or apologetic. The polemics, generally written by lawyers, sociologists, and journalists more or less hostile to the establishment, assume or assert that large corporations and major government organizations are prescient, powerful, and relentlessly self-serving, and attribute this potency in large measure to the influence and manipulative abilities of their legal advisers. Apart from its bias, this literature often suffers from an internally inconsistent attitude toward the problem of responsibility. On the one hand, economic determinism is relied on to show that the actors involved are prisoners of role and therefore incapable of ethical autonomy even if they wished to express it. On the other hand, primitive concepts of moral responsibility are relied on to condemn failures to live up to professed ethical norms. The apologetics mostly originate in the practicing bar. They treat the relationship between a large organization and its legal counsel as being like that between a sole practitioner and the "individual client" who is the bar's idealized version of its clientele. Further, they often exhibit a myopic self-assurance that the lawyer's definition of the lawyer-client relationship fulfills client expectations, and is an appropraite concept of professional probity, and is good for the general public interest. So far apart are these bodies of literature that if one compares the most violent polemics with the most self-righteous apologetics, it becomes unclear whether a single subject is under consideration.

It would seem that a serious assessment of the professional ethics of lawyers must reject three assumptions that are commonly made in discussions of the subject. One is that the practitioner is a consummate manipulator who can shape his environment to avoid situations that might cause him difficulty. This assumption is made not only about lawyers but about doctors (they set up the tests and treatments), journalists (they control public opinion), businessmen (they control markets), though not social critics (we do not control the culture). This assumption can be rejected because it is not true, at least in the unqualified way that some critics suggest. Furthermore, to the extent that manipulation is possible the ethical problem is simply pushed one step backward to that of the ethics of manipulation. A second assumption is that the practitioner is simply a functionary in the system and hence disengaged from the ethical aspects of his vocation. This assumption is either false, for the reason that alternative vocations are open to lawyers, or question-begging, because it defines the lawyer's function in a way that frees him of ethical burdens in what he does. The third assumption is that the practitioner in the "power structure" is simply indifferent to what others might perceive as ethical issues concerning his role. The Seven Springs discussion, unless it was merely a charade, is evidence to the contrary. The elite lawyer may be tough and clever, and a creature of his environment like the rest of us, but he is concerned about being, as well as seeming to be, an honorable person.

Fortunately, there have appeared sober and serious examinations that do not rest on such simplistic premises. Competent social scientists and journalists such as Jerome Carlin, Douglas Rosenthal, Erwin Smigel, and Martin Mayer have provided us with valuable external assessments. In the academic branch of the legal profession a literature on the ethics of the profession is emerging.[3] The American Bar

3. Among other works there are now several well-conceived coursebooks, including Countryman, Finman, and Schneyer, *The Lawyer in Modern Society* (2d ed. 1976); Kaufman, *Problems in Professional Responsibility* (1976); Mellinkoff, *Lawyers and the System of Justice* (1976); Morgan and Rotunda, *Professional Responsibility* (1976); Redlich, *Professional Responsibility: A Problem Approach* (1976).

Foundation, research affiliate of the American Bar Association, has become a center for the systematic study of the profession and its functions. The organized bar has become increasingly candid and objective in its attitude toward the ethical dilemmas arising in the practice of law.[4] This book aspires to contribute to that stream of thought.

4. See, e.g., Ass'n. Bar City of N.Y., *Professional Responsibility of the Lawyer, The Murky Divide Between Right and Wrong* (1976).

1. An Ethical Lawyer

In much of literature the idea of an ethical lawyer is regarded as a contradiction in terms. Thus Shakespeare: "quiddities... and tricks"; "the first thing we do, let's kill all the lawyers." Thus Burke: "It is not what a lawyer tells me I may do; but what humanity, reason, and justice, tell me I ought to do." Thus Sandburg: "Why is there always a secret singing when a lawyer cashes in?" Thus Judge Learned Hand: "About trials hang a suspicion of trickery and a sense of a result depending upon cajolery or worse." Folklore and popular opinion similarly reflect deep, probably ineradicable suspicion of lawyers' honesty and integrity. Even within the legal profession an ethically exemplary lawyer is probably taken to be an idealization rather than a descriptive category.

This book, however, is about an ethical lawyer. It assumes that someone can be ethical while being a lawyer, but is an inquiry into the sense and context in which this assumption might be sustained. The inquiry ought therefore to begin by stating what is meant by *ethics*. As used here, *ethics* refers to imperatives regarding the welfare of others that are recognized as binding upon a person's conduct in some more immediate and binding sense than *law* and in some more general and impersonal sense than *morals*. This definition is narrower than those of the philosophers. At least in some such definitions, law, morals, and ethics are a part of a general subject that includes all aspects of the concept of obligation. Moreover, among the various systems of ethics there are ones that deny the existence or even the intelligibility of an imperative regarding the welfare of others. In these systems, the sense of self is the only thing that can or should be given regard or, indeed, the only thing that can be said to exist. But in these systems it also seems impossible coherently to condemn another person's conduct as unethical, which is the problem that both lawyers and their ethical critics are concerned with. So, while acknowledging the place in the philosophical universe of what are termed ethical egoism and radical ethical passivity, our concern here is with the relationships between rules that are believed to exist and the conduct they are thought to refer to.

Even when this is taken as a place of beginning, there remain serious questions as to what ethical rules are all about. For example, they can be regarded as moral sentiments that have attained a certain publicity and formality but which remain matters of personal taste and conviction, like preferences in art. On the other hand, they can be regarded as a subspecies of legislation—rules that differ from law only in that their enforcement is relatively informal. On another plane, ethics can be considered a process of subjective deliberation leading to a decision about what one ought to do, or as an interpersonal exchange establishing what a group will say one should have done. Perhaps in the world of acting, judging, and being judged, ethics is best regarded as all of these—deliberation about how one should act given the existence of rules established by a concensus that one shares substantially if not unreservedly. But if this is ethics, how does it differ from law? Is it not simply a subspecies of legislation, having the sanction of authority and the pragmatic value of protecting order and autonomy, but not entailing any special moral obligation?

This leads to a second problem, peculiar to legal ethics. A lawyer is a legal technician. His training demythologizes the law and exposes his mind to the ambiguities of its commands, the frequently specious character of its policy, and the frailties of its interpreters. His professional function consists largely of providing counsel for clients about how to escape or mitigate the incidence of the law's obligations, or, if he is in law enforcement or activist law reform, on how to make the incidence of the law enforcement broader and deeper. The essence of these activities is the manipulation of governmental authority and the language and social processes through which that authority is exercised. The lawyer as counselor gives at least lip service to the idea that the law's obligations are real, but he is bound to advise on the extent to which they are mere formalities or even less. What view should he take of rules that address his own conduct? Are they legal regulations whose burdens he may minimize or obviate by technical advice delivered professionally to himself, or are they stricutres of conscience whose only meaning is in their observation?

Finally, the notion of ethics as applied to lawyers entails the difficulty, common to all professions, arising from the fact that there is a client in the picture. Ethics, seriously discussed as in philosophy, usually speak in terms that require treating all other persons on an equal footing. That is, their norms are cast as universals in which in principle every "other" is entitled to equal rcspect and consideration in the calculation of the actor's alternatives and course of action. On the other hand, professional ethics give priority to an "other" who is a client and in general require subordination of everyone else's interests to that of the client. Indeed, the central problem in professional ethics can be described as the tension between the client's preferred position resulting from the professional connection and the position of equality that everyone else is accorded by general principles of morality and legality.

In the discussions at Seven Springs none of these difficulties was addressed in terms, but they all intruded in the course of the interchange. By way of an orderly beginning of the discussion, an attempt was made to describe the nature of the ethical norms from the viewpoint of a conscientious lawyer. This description was conspicuous in its antiformalism.

Professional ethics, it was said, should be seen as general principles of conduct, not a corpus of specific rules; as a group of principles that conflict with each other in many applications and extensions, not an internally consistent code; as qualified imperatives that always have to yield at some point to competing considerations; as resultants of encounters with tough practical choices in real life, not abstract mandates laid down in advance; as products of personal deliberation, not emanations from some outside authority; as the expression of self-fulfillment and self-control, not subordinancy to external discipline. When the discussion developed, the same concept was suggested in less analytic and more allusive terms: "civility," "ethically pragmatic," "no Mickey Mouse," the conduct of a "decent human being."

This complex and ineffable concept of ethics defies formal statement. It may evidence a mentality that is opportunistic, manipulative, self-protective, and hypocritical. It may also evidence a mentality that is sensitive to subtle differences between ethically problematic situations, to small variations in relationships that call for quite different courses of action, and to the fact that pretending to govern one's conduct solely by reference to rules is either self-deceptive or a pretense. In any event, a relativist concept of ethics does not necessarily indicate a relativist attitude about the importance of ethics. While it could be the confession of one who is indifferent to the virtue of his conduct, it could also be the affirmation of one who is sufficiently confident of his capacity for virtue that he does not feel impelled to make the Pharisee's display. And the patterns of behavior to which a theory of ethics might lead are equally ambiguous.

There are other conceptions of ethical rules. One quite

different conception is what might be called ethical legalism. This conception treats rules as definite and knowable imperatives that one has a moral obligation to obey. In the modern "realist" era, this view of ethical rules is widely regarded as naive and perhaps even fatuous, but it has substance if taken seriously. Stated in sympathetic terms legal ethics in this approach could be considered as follows:

The office of lawyer has a legally definite character. It originates with the fact that a person can act as a lawyer only by governmental license issued after a prescribed course of training and demonstration of proficiency by formal examination. The office has defined functions, principally those of advocate before the courts and other adjudicative tribunals and the giving of advice about what the law is. The performance of these functions involves complex interactions between the lawyer, his client, other parties, and the courts. These interactions influence the quality of administered justice and the security of citizens in their legal relationships. How the lawyer's function should be conducted admits a wide range of possibility, over which historically and contemporarily there is much debate and difference of opinion, even among persons of admitted good will and personal integrity. The matter cannot satisfactorily be left to individual conscience or vaguely articulated "traditions of the profession." Hence, it is appropriate and socially necessary that regulations authoritatively resolve the debated issues, so that both lawyers and others have a common understanding of expected and permissible behavior in performance of the lawyer's office. Legal ethics thus is properly a matter of positive law of the same character as laws governing a regulated business. While the requirements of such a positive law are not the only normative considerations by which a lawyer might guide his conduct, they are minimum standards in that a lawyer should at all events comply with them.

This approach to legal ethics is expressed in the legal

profession's Code of Professional Responsibility adopted by the American Bar Association in 1970. The Code, whose provisions are considered in a subsequent chapter, contains three types of ethical statements. One consists of "Canons," which are brief, hortatory generalizations of which the following are illustrative:

"A lawyer should preserve the confidences and secrets of a client." (Canon 4)

"A lawyer should represent a client zealously within the bounds of the law." (Canon 7)

The second type of statement in the Code is called an "Ethical Consideration." The various "ethical considerations" include reasons and explanations for the ethical rules and also guides that a lawyer may consider in making the ethical assessments that are within his personal discretion.

The essential corpus of the Code, however, is a body of statute-like rules, printed in boldface type, called the Disciplinary Rules. They state rules of conduct whose violation is supposed to be a proper basis for such sanctions as reprimand, suspension, or disbarment. According to the Code, if a lawyer's conduct violates one of the Disciplinary Rules, it is unethical as a matter of law, even if it might be right or justified when considered in terms of the relativistic and more amorphous approach to ethics that has been earlier described.

It is not easy to summarize the lawyers' attitudes toward the Code, if indeed they could be said to share a single attitude. If the Seven Sprints participants' attitudes are indicative, lawyers clearly consider the Code's provisions significant. They knew what the Code said (which is not true of all lawyers), they recognized that it had the force of law, and they accepted, perhaps with qualifications, that they were bound by it. They also concurred, at least on some level

AN ETHICAL LAWYER   7

of generality, with its most critical stipulations—that a lawyer must not disclose confidential statements made to him by his client, that he must not "assist his client in conduct that the lawyer knows to be illegal or fraudulent" [Disciplinary Rule 7-102(a)(7)], and that "neither his personal interests, the interests of other clients, nor the desires of third persons should be permitted to dilute his loyalty to his client" (Ethical Consideration 5-1). On the other hand, they were less than entirely comfortable with the orientation and tenor of the Code, to put it mildly: "Made for downstate Illinois in the 1860s"; a "hodgepodge"; "never applicable in the real world"; "evasive and pretentious."

Their dissatisfaction was in some respects quite specific, centering on certain problems that will be considered later on, including these:

— The Code does not provide standards for determining who is the client; it simply assumes that the client is readily identifiable.
— Except in one or two isolated contexts, the Code does not deal with situations in which legal advice is being provided by a firm or other group of lawyers rather than an individual practitioner; it assumes that the same rules can apply to both.
— The Code does not deal directly with the lawyer's role when he acts otherwise than as an advocate or a giver of advice, for example when he is negotiator, mediator, or trustee.
— Several rules of the Code presuppose a distinction between a past transaction, first brought to the lawyer after it has occurred, and a future transaction, in which the lawyer advises or assists in a course of action still in contemplation. In reality, events of the past, present, and future are often inseparable.
— In certain applications, the Code's provisions contradict

what the participants understood to be the ethical lawyer's proper course of action.

At a somewhat different level, there was dissatisfaction with the Code's conception of how an ethical lawyer should approach certain dilemmas. One of these is conflict of interest—conflict between different clients served by the same lawyer or firm of lawyers, and conflict between the lawyer or firm of lawyers and the client himself (or "itself," because most of the discussion concerned organizational clients). The Code holds, as indicated by Ethical Consideration 5-1, that such conflicts should be avoided. However, it permits a lawyer to act for a client with whom he has a conflict of interest, or to act concurrently for clients between whom there is a conflict of interest, when the client has given "consent after full disclosure." The ultimate source of dissatisfaction with this position, which is explored later on, is that the relationship between lawyer and client, like any human relationship, is shot through with conflict; the sensitive handling of such conflict requires both more and less than "full disclosure."

Another source of dissatisfaction is that the Code treats the lawyer's immediate constituency as being divided into only three basic categories: courts and judges; clients; and others. To courts and judges is owed the duty of being an "officer of the court," whatever that might mean. To clients is owed almost unqualified loyalty. To others, whoever they may be, is owed whatever is not incompatible with the duty to a client. The category of "others," however, includes people having a wide variety of relationships to the lawyer's client. Thus "others" include opponents in litigation; opposite numbers in negotiating situations; persons having interests distinct from but parallel to those of the client; employees of a client; members of a client's family; customers and stockholders of a client; persons having secondary dealings with the client; and in some contexts "the public." It simply cannot be that all these relationships are satisfactorily governed by the same ethical rubric, but that is in general the posture of the Code.

Still another source of dissatisfaction was the ambivalence of the Code on the priorities to be assigned to its rules when they contradict each other in application. When a lawyer discovers that his client is engaged in a course of continuing conduct that may constitute a crime, is he governed by the rule that he should preserve his client's secrets or the rule that he should not assist his client in conduct that is illegal?

These kinds of difficulties with the Code can be considered technical inadequacies in draftmanship, failures authoritatively to resolve important issues on which there might be disagreement. But they may reflect a more serious shortcoming, that the Code was based on a simplistic conception of the processes it purports to regulate.

A deeper dissatisfaction with the Code emerged, and in a peculiar way. Several of the participants observed that their clients—sophisticated businessmen—thought the lawyers' rules were simply devices for the self-protection of lawyers. This is a common suspicion and a justified one, for even a mild skeptic would suppose that a profession's code of ethics would be somewhat self-protective. However, the rules that businessmen see as lawyers' self-protection were not those that are usually identified as such—for example rules against advertising and rules giving licensed lawyers a monopoly of all services that the lawyers define as "legal." Rather, the criticism had to do with some of the central ethical rules, particularly the rule that a lawyer may not represent conflicting interests.

According to the rule book, a lawyer may represent clients whose interests conflict only if he obtains their consent upon "full disclosure"; if he cannot make "full disclosure" because such a disclosure to one client would be injurious to the other, then under the code he must step aside and represent neither. Corporate officers see this rule as a device whereby a lawyer can refuse to get involved when a conflict within the corporation becomes really serious. They don't see why one client and possibly both, at the moment of their greatest need, should lose the assistance of the lawyer best informed of the situation. One participant asked, "As a decent human being, can you really do that?" Another rejoined, "No, you accept the conflict and do the best you can for both."

Thus, these lawyers, at least in some circumstances, would rather bank on the clients' faith in them, run the risk of mistrust and subsequent recrimination, and act, than take refuge in the Code's inhibitions. That is, they think an ethical lawyer's responsibilities include running ethical risks, not only the risk of violating the Code of Professional Responsibility, but also the risk inherent in making choices that could result in harm to the clients they are pledged to serve. More than that, they think anyone who cannot endure those risks cannot properly serve his clients.

This attitude can be viewed as the self-righteousness of a professional elite that considers itself above the law laid down for practitioners of less stature. It can be viewed, in stronger condemnation, as an escape mechanism dressed in ethical pretention, allowing lawyers to keep on serving clients who pay good fees. But this detachment regarding the Code is open to another interpretation. It can be viewed as a recognition of a duty of civil disobedience, a willingness to violate positive law with full consciousness of the potential consequences of doing so. Many of these lawyers appeared to feel that discernment in professional ethics not only permits but requires such disobedience on proper occasion. Perhaps their feeling was strengthened by their confidence that, in the unlikely event of their being called to account, their reputations in the profession would see them through. If so, then only a member of a professional elite ordinarily has that kind of confidence and is therefore in a position to pursue such a course of action.

There is a paradox in all this. If the profession were uniformly an elite, it would be unlikely to have adopted a formal code and so the problem of disobeying it would not arise. Our relatively heterogeneous legal profession, however, seems to require positive legislation to resolve questions of conduct about which there is not a consensus. But positive legislation is inevitably simplistic to some degree, and thus an incomplete guide in delicate situations. A truly conscientious and self-confident practitioner would not feel bound to follow the letter of the law when his personal judgment dictated a different course. Hence, the concept of a principled violation of the rules of ethics introduces what is in fact a triple standard—conscience for some, code for others, and lip-service for still others. The point is not that this is a desirable state of affairs, but a state of affairs that necessarily results from the admission that conduct can be at the same time unlawful and right. And this returns us to the relativistic conception of ethics with which the participants began.

Another aspect of the question whether there can be an ethical lawyer appears in the disjunction of two ideas, one concerning the idea of "being" ethical and the other concerning the professional functions of lawyers.

As to the idea of being ethical: Ethical rules, like legal and moral rules, combine an element of approval or disapproval with an element of neutrality. The element of approval or disapproval is clear enough: Stealing is bad, betraying a trust is bad, being an accomplice to a crime is bad; fulfilling a contract is good, being helpful to the poor is good, paying the due amount of one's taxes is good, etc. The element of neutrality is less apparent. It arises from the fact that the approving or disapproving statements in ethical rules (or legal or moral rules) are expressed in categorical and abstract terms, referring not to specific instances but to types of instances.

Thus, rules condemn stealing without indicating whether an individual instance of behavior *is* stealing, and approve fulfilling a contract without indicating that a specific contract was fulfilled. Rules go on to provide definitions of the kinds of things that are condemned and approved. The definitions can be more or less particularized. But no matter how particularized, the definitions are generalizations that apply to all situations coming within their terms. In the Biblical phrase, a rule is "no respecter of persons," that is, it is neutral among them.

To say that a particular person is "ethical" or "unethical," however, is to make a very particularized statement—indeed an intensely personal one. What is meant by such a statement is not that the person was or was not governed by ethical rules, but that he conducted himself in a way that displays a good or bad attitude or predisposition toward conformity to rules. The evaluation of a person's ethical standing is based on the assumption that he has had a choice between obedience and violation and that he reveals himself in the choices he makes.

Judgments of a person's ethical nature are of course tempered by recognition of special circumstances. Although the rules of behavior are framed in universal terms, only in a rigorous system taken seriously is there an expectation that they will be applied in that way. In folk ethics it is accepted that a person owes one kind of duty to a member of his family (or village or working group) and another to those with whom his relationship is more remote. However, when the possibility of such discrimination is sanctioned, it immediately opens up all kinds of questions along at least two lines: How does one rank the various "others" (spouse, child, cousin, next-door neighbor, fellow worker, compatriot, etc.) and how does one rank different kinds of obligations (to refrain from killing, to refrain from stealing, to forbear, to counsel forebearance by others, to come to another's aid, to sacrifice one's self for another, etc.). These questions pose great philosophic difficulties for all universalistic ethical conceptions, a fact that may explain why these conceptions are usually expressed in wholly abstract terms. They pose similar difficulties in practical application, so that folk ethics is a mishmash of homilies, legalistic formulations of various duty relationships, and resignation to subjective ethical choice.

We lead our daily lives by making ethical discriminations in these terms, but we are left defenseless against charges of inconsistency, casuistry, and discrimination. The burden of these charges can be lifted by attributing responsibility to the force of circumstances. Thus we say that no one volunteers to have to distinguish between his spouse and child, employer and customer, or neighbor and the building inspector. When events conscript us into doing so, we make ethical distinctions because we must in order to continue to function. At the level of principle, therefore, ethics consists of universals, while at the level of application it is a complicated scheme of excuses based on practical necessity.

The rules governing a lawyer's office are neither. They are not universal because they give a preferred position to clients; the office of lawyer begins with having to make distinctions among persons. At least in an immediate sense, they are not based on practical necessity, for no one is compelled to become a lawyer and, ordinarily at least, no lawyer is compelled to take a particular case. While in some situations a lawyer is supposed to act with perfect neutrality among others, a lawyer usually intervenes in relationships between others with a predisposition to treat the one who is his client with greater solicitude than he treats the other, regardless of the merits of their respective positions.

According to any "nonlegal" ethics, intervention on these terms is difficult to justify. It violates the principle of equal treatment inherent in all forms of universalist ethics. It lacks the involuntarism that is present in the ethical dilemmas of everyday life. For the lawyer does not merely encounter choices between the conflicting interests of others but makes a business out of such encounters, and takes partisan positions for money. Thus, his vocation violates the concepts of ethics held both by philosophers and in folklore. On this analysis, the idea of an ethical lawyer is therefore an impossibility.

2. The Official Rules

Every organized profession has rules of professional conduct. In purpose, style, and content, codes of ethics differ from one profession to another and have varied over the course of history. In the older professions they appear to have originated as exhortations to initiates upon completion of apprenticeship, something like commencement addresses or oaths of office. They persisted in this form until modern times and in some professions still do. Thus, the medical profession adheres to the Hippocratic oath and the military punishes "conduct unbecoming an officer." This kind of code emphasizes the profession's public service ideal and the fraternal relationship among its members and leaves it largely unsaid how the profession was to be practiced. It is assumed that this would be learned through an apprenticeship over which the established members of the profession had control.

The typical professional code of ethics presupposes that the profession has exclusive or substantial control over the process by which professional competence is attained and verified. It presupposes that its members practice in a milieu in which their competence and integrity is a matter of reputation among their professional colleagues and clientele, and that professional reputation must be maintained by good practice as a matter of professional survival. It also presupposes that a profession is something like a partnership in that a member can be disciplined or excluded on grounds that the professional company deems sufficient.

In such a context, an ethical code need not be a legal definition of terms on which the profession may be practiced. It can be merely an admonition that there should be compliance with definitions supplied by precept and example. When a question of professional propriety has arisen, the code may serve the function of legitimating judgments concerning whether unprofessional conduct has occurred. But the judgments themselves are based on unverbalized norms handed from one professional generation to another.

All this has changed a good deal over the past century. In varying degrees the active members of the old professions have lost direct control over the process by which basic professional competence is attained and verified. These functions have been assumed by career educators who prescribe and administer professional school curricula and by other specialists who prescribe and administer the examinations for admission to the profession. The typical milieu of practice is no longer a small community of practitioners in a proportionately small community of potential clientele—downstate Illinois in the 1860s—but an array of practitioners diffused throughout a metropolis. Hence, compared with the past, the controlling influence of general reputation within a local profession and community has been greatly attenuated. Moreover, to an increasing degree the practitioner operates within an organization, such as a law firm or hospital, in which his own individual competence and integrity are at the same time difficult to distinguish from that of the organization and subject to the influence of the organization's own norms of competence and integrity. (These norms may, of course, be much more exacting than those of the community at large.) Thus the older mechanisms of fraternal control by the profession at large and of community control through individual reputation, which undergirded hortatory ethical codes, now appear to be much less influential than they once were.

Paralleling the decline of informal fraternal and community controls on professionals is the intensified involvement of the state in the regulation of the professions. Today, the right of persons pursuing a particular vocation to call themselves professionals originates in statute, along with the rights to prohibit others from holding themselves out as members of the profession, to establish educational and examination requirements, to regulate professional competition, to specify standards of competence and integrity, and to impose sanctions for misconduct. Not only in the new professions but in the old ones as well, the bodies that govern a profession are no longer exclusively selected by its members as in a private association. Rather, appointment of these bodies is through concurrent authority, in one form or another, of the profession and the government. The professional authority may, for example, be appointed by a state official on nomination by the profession or, as in the legal profession, consist of a combination of professional officials (the bar association) and a state agency (the courts). In addition, regulation of the professions increasingly partakes of administrative law, that is, the law regulating how the state may engage in regulation. Among the principles of administrative law are that the regulations governing the activity in question be specified in advance and that they provide intelligible definitions of prohibited conduct. To conform to these requirements, the rules governing a profession have to be something else than a statement of ideals and aspirations; they have to be a body of law.

There is thus a disharmony between the rhetoric of a professional oath of office and the rhetoric of a regulatory code. This corresponds to an underlying disharmony between the concept of a profession as a self-regulating band of gentle persons engaged in public service and the concept of a profession as a regulated vocation. The fraternal connections remain strong and thus far governance of the professions has not been fully assimilated to the regulation of an industry.

Probably it never will be. On the other hand, there are increasing pressures toward formal regulation. These include direct governmental controls on the professions and indirect ones such as externally imposed standards of professional malpractice. Moreover, most professionals are now subject to sources of influence by persons and institutions on whom they are economically dependent but with whom they do not have a traditional practitioner-client relationship. Thus professionals have to deal with employers (law firms, accountancy firms, hospitals, government agencies), large institutional clients (corporations, unions), and insurers (medical and dental insurance, liability insurance underwriters). The very number and strength of these competing influences is itself a powerful impetus to transforming the concept of a code of professional ethics from a generalized statement of ideals into a set of specific rules by which the competing demands on the professionals are reconciled.

The regulatory motif is conspicuous in the legal profession's Code of Professional Responsibility. The history of the code reflects its evolution from oath of office to something like a statute.[1] Until the nineteenth century the bar was governed only by oral "traditions of the profession." In the mid-nineteenth century, there were efforts to reduce these traditions to writing, notably in lectures by Judge George Sharswood of Pennsylvania, entitled "The Aims and Duties of the Profession of the Law." Judge Sharswood's exposition had considerable system but in tenor it was still admonitory and it was intended as an address to young lawyers newly admitted to the bar. The lectures proved to be the nucleus of a more formal statement of rules adopted at the beginning of the twentieth century. At that point the American Bar Association promulgated its Canons of Professional Ethics,

---

1. There is a valuable historical bibliography in Mellinkoff, *The Conscience of a Lawyer* 275-293 (1972).

drawing heavily on Judge Sharswood. The Canons were still more systematic and detailed and undertook to deal dispositively with certain then much-disputed issues, such as whether a lawyer has an obligation to act as advocate for a client with whose cause he has no sympathy. On the other hand, they were still largely hortatory in character, as is suggested by the term "canons" and by the fact that they were intended for adoption as the rules of the profession and not as public law.

In 1970 the American Bar Association adoped the Code of Professional Responsibility.[2] This document undertook to state comprehensively the rules by which lawyers should perform their calling. As noted earlier, it consists of three different kinds of norms—general concepts, exhortations, and "Disciplinary Rules." The latter consist of imperatives formulated in the form of administrative regulations and were designed for adoption by appropriate legal authority with the binding effect of law. The Code indeed has been so adopted, sometimes with amendments, in most of the states.

The Code of Professional Responsibility is a complex document. It governs several matters that are very important to the public interest but irrelevant to the present discussion. These include:

— Rules regulating competition among lawyers (advertising, solicitation, etc.), which are subsumed under the rubric of assisting "the legal profession in fulfilling its duty to make legal counsel available."
— Rules regulating competition from outside the profession. The substance of these rules is that lawyers should prevent nonlawyers from doing anything that is the "practice of law," whatever that may include.

---

2. On the Code, see Wright, "The Code of Professional Responsibility: Its History and Objectives," 24 *Ark. L. Rev.* 1 (1970).

- Rules requiring that a lawyer practice competently. Technical competence is presupposed in the present discussion.
- Certain special rules having to do with lawyers who hold public office, whose substance is that a lawyer should not use public office for the benefit of private clients, or take bribes.

Putting these aside, the Code's rules of professional conduct deal with essentially three problems:

- Confidentiality: What matters learned by a lawyer should he treat as secret, and from whom, and under what conditions may the secrecy be lifted?
- Conflict of Interest: When and to what extent is a lawyer prohibited from acting because there is a conflict of interest between his clients or between himself and a client?
- Prohibited assistance: What kinds of things is a lawyer prohibited from doing for a client?

These are all tough problems, and not only for lawyers. What is perhaps not fully appreciated, by lawyers and laymen alike, is that similar problems arise in everyday life. If this fact were appreciated by lawyers, they might be able to perceive and to discuss the problems free of the introverted assumption that lawyers alone can appreciate their complex and stressful nature. If laymen recognized the similarity, they might regard the lawyers' ethical dilemmas with greater comprehension and perhaps even greater sympathy.

Many illustrations might be suggested from other walks of life, at work and at home, of problems involving confidentiality, conflict of interest, and prohibited assistance. A few will suffice to make the point. Thus, regarding confidentiality: What should a parent do who knows that his child has stolen something from a store? A pediatrician who discovers physical abuse of a child by its parents? A teacher who finds out that a student has been using drugs? An accountant who knows that his client is understating income for tax purposes? Regarding conflict of interest: Does a parent send a healthy child to college rather than send a sick one to the Mayo Clinc? A plant manager trim on safety systems to keep his company financially afloat? A doctor order hospitalization because medical insurance will not otherwise cover the patient? A supervisor commend a subordinate who may become a rival? Regarding prohibited assistance: Do you help a friend by lying to the police? Omit adverse information when asked to evaluate a former student or employee? Help sell stock that may be overvalued? Maintain the "character of a neighborhood" by not renting to a black?

If there is any peculiarity about these problems as they are confronted by lawyers, it is that a lawyer confronts them every day and is supposed to resolve them in a fashion that is compatible with a conception of his professional role. The Code of Professional Responsibility undertakes to tell him how he should do so.

Confidentiality

The basic rule of confidentiality is that the lawyer should keep everything secret that he learns from or about a "client," except when its disclosure helps his client. The Disciplinary Rules do not quite put it in that way. However, if the rules are analyzed in the contexts in which they apply, their practical effect is to require blanket secrecy unless giving out information will advance the client's interest.

In terms, the rules governing preservation of a client's secrets refer to two types of confidential matters: Communications received *from* the client in the course of the attoney-client relationship, as defined in the attorney-client privilege; and information *about* the client that might be "embarrassing or . . . detrimental" to the client.[3]

The attorney-client privilege is defined by rules of law outside the Code of Professional Responsibility, by a subcategory of the law of evidence. This body of law has considerable technical intricacy all its own.[4] The attoney-client privilege strictly speaking has application only in a forensic setting, that is, in a trial or something like it such as a legislative investigation. The privilege comes into play when a demand is made on a lawyer in a trial or hearing that he reveal information gained from his client. The rule is that the lawyer must refuse to comply with the demand if he thinks the information is within the privilege and not excluded by one of the exceptions to it. When the lawyer makes such a refusal, the court or other tribunal then has to decide whether the claim of privilege is valid. If the court rules that the claim is valid, the lawyer does not have to provide the information and that is the end of the matter. However, if the court rules that the privilege does not apply, the lawyer faces a difficult problem: Should he comply with the demand or persist in refusing to make the disclosure, thus running the risk of being held in contempt of court?

Although this predicament is one of extreme distress for the lawyer, he does not reach it until he has been given a ruling by the tribunal that the claim of privilege is unwarranted. As a guide to his conduct up until that point, therefore, the rule of attorney-client privilege has at least superficial simplicity: A lawyer should not accede to any tribunal's

3. The Code rule on disclosure of a client's "confidences and secrets" is DR 4-101.
4. On the evidentiary privilege against disclosure by an attorney of matters related to him by his client, see Cleary et al., *McCormick's Evidence* c. 10 (2d ed. 1972).

demand for disclosure of information about his client unless he thinks the information is helpful to or at least neutral in its effects on the client. As we shall see presently, the lawyer's other responsibilities to a client may require him to consider whether waiving the privilege would be advantageous, itself often a difficult question. However, unless it appears that there is some such advantage to be gained, he makes no disclosure.

The other type of confidential matter is information that might be "embarrassing or detrimental to" the client, whether it is learned from the client or from other sources. This definition is supplied by the Code of Professional Responsibility itself and is a very broad one. Almost any information has potential for injury, unless it is unequivocally favorable or empty of detail or simply trivial. A prudent lawyer would not take it upon himself to guess whether something would be sufficiently innocuous to pass this test. He therefore keeps secret everything he knows about his client, except in two situations: that in which saying something would work to the client's advantage; and that in which the matter falls within special exceptions to the duty to maintain confidentiality.

It can often be to the client's advantage to lift secrecy, sometimes even about matters that the client could not be compelled to disclose.[5] For example, when a person is prosecuted for a crime he cannot be compelled to testify against himself. Nevertheless, if a client faces the possibility that a prosecution may be brought, it may be to his advantage to make a full voluntary disclosure in the excepta-

---

5. Often the client is under practical compulsion to make disclosures, for example to an auditor in order to obtain a "clean" audit report. For the difficulties this can pose when the client's lawyer has to make a response on behalf of the client, see American Bar Ass'n., *Statement of Policy Regarding Lawyers' Responses to Auditors' Requests for Information* (January 15, 1976).

tion that the prosecution will conclude that no crime has been committed or at least that a criminal prosecution would be unwarranted. Similarly, a client facing a civil lawsuit in which he has strong exonerating evidence can sometimes avoid being sued by voluntarily making the evidence available to the person who is threatening to sue him.

This kind of possibility is relevant to one of the special exceptions to the lawyer's duty to maintain the secrets of his client. The exception is that the lawyer may waive the attorney-client privilege in a court, or disclose a client's secret out of court, if the client consents to his doing so. In operation, this is usually the same thing as saying that a lawyer should make a disclosure of confidential matter when it helps the client. This is because the lawyer who is called on to make a disclosure is usually also the one who advises the client whether to consent to the disclosure. The lawyer or adviser thus suggests whether the client should consent, the client directs the lawyer accordingly, and the lawyer then discloses or not, depending on what his advice was. Hence, the effect of the exception is only to make the important point that the lawyer ordinarily should not disclose a client's secret without the client's consent; the decision whether the consent should be given will be strongly influenced if not wholly induced by the lawyer's own advice to the client.

There is a situation in which application of the disclosure-with-consent rule is more complicated. This is where the lawyer has two clients whose interests may conflict, a situation that recurs all the time in the practice of large independent law firms. The rule is that the lawyer may act for both clients only if each is given "full disclosure" and then consents to the dual representation. But to give "full disclosure" requires that each client be told things about the other. These may include secrets that the lawyer supposedly may not reveal. A Catch-22 dilemma is thus posed: The lawyer can act only after he discloses, but in order to disclose he has to reveal the identity of the other client and at least the general nature of the latter's conflicting interest. Furthermore, the practical inconsistency between the rule of secrecy and the rule requiring disclosure works out to be reciprocal: The fuller the disclosure to one client, the greater the revelation of the secrets of the other. As we shall see, this poses special difficulty for a law firm that represents big corporate clients, because such a firm runs into the problem all the time.

The second exception to the rule of confidentiality concerns disclosure of wrongful acts by the client. The terms of this exception are complicated by the fact that the rule of attorney-client privilege was developed by the courts and is considerably different from the rule of confidentiality in the profession's Code of Professional Responsibility. According to the rule of attorney-client privilege, a lawyer can be required to disclose facts he has learned from his client indicating that the client contemplates commission of a crime or a fraud. Thus, while a lawyer cannot be compelled to reveal *past* wrongs by his client, he can be compelled to reveal intended wrongful acts if they would constitute a crime or a fraud. The critical elements are thus futurity and legal wrongfulness. However, as noted earlier, the attorney-client privilege comes into operation only when a court or other tribunal asks a lawyer to disclose information about his client; the lawyer need not volunteer information about his client's intended wrong-doing. As a practical matter, a court has to have found out about the wrong-doing from some other source, and thereby realize that questioning the lawyer might provide additional evidence. As a result, from the viewpoint of the lawyer the exception to the attorney-client privilege allows him to remain silent if he has knowledge that his client plans a crime or fraud, except in the unlikely event of his being asked about the matter by a court.

From a practical standpoint, therefore, the important exception regarding confidentiality is the one in the Code of

Professional Responsibility, for this is the rule that applies to the lawyer in his office, so to speak. Prior to 1974 the rule seemed to be as follows: A lawyer was authorized but not required to reveal secrets of his client in order to prevent a future crime and was required to reveal secrets of his client in order to rectify a fraud committed by his client. Under this rule, a lawyer who discovered a "fraud" by his client had to try to persuade his client to rectify it and, failing that, to report the fraud to the injured person. The rule applied to a past fraud and probably also to a fraud in the planning stage, certainly so after it actually go under way. Hence, for example, a lawyer who discovered that his client's issue of stock was fraudulently overvalued, or that his client had committed a fraud in selling the stock, would have to report the client.

The rule appears to have stood this way since adoption of the Canon of Professional Ethics in 1908. There were conflicting interpretations that made it unclear whether the duty to prevent fraud and crime prevailed over the duty of confidentiality. Furthermore, the scope of the duty to reveal fraud was gradually narrowed by changes in the law that had nothing directly to do with the Canons of Ethics. In recent times, various kinds of fraud have been made a crime as well as a civil wrong, such as fraud committed by use of the mail, fraud in sale of securities, fraud in real estate speculation, and so on. Every time a kind of fraud was made a crime, it ceased to be one that a lawyer was obliged to report and became one merely that he could report without being guilty of unethical conduct.

Nevertheless, the exception to the rule of confidentiality sometimes clearly required a lawyer to "blow the whistle" on his client. This apparently was regarded as an intolerable obligation. In 1974 the Code of Professional Responsibility accordingly was amended, through an amendment, it might be said, whose effect can be discerned only by one skillful in following cross-references and double negatives (that is, a lawyer). Under the amended rule, reporting an intended crime remained optional for a lawyer. With respect to frauds that are not crimes, the Code was changed substantially if indirectly by providing that the duty to report does not apply if it would involve violating the rule of confidentiality. This of course eviscerated the duty to report fraud: The rule of confidentiality prohibits disclosing anything that is embarrassing to the client and fraud is always embarrassing.[6]

The rule in the Code of Professional Responsibility regarding disclosure of client frauds and crimes thus reduces itself to a very modest exception to the rule of secrecy: A lawyer may—but is not ethically required to—report on a client who is planning a crime. Even the option to report a client who intends to commit a crime is narrow in scope, particularly as applied to business activities that may violate the criminal law. This is because, while there is an option to report intended crimes, there is a duty to withhold information about past crimes. Whether the lawyer can make a disclosure of a crime by his client thus depends on a distinction between past and future crimes.

The distinction between past and future is difficult to maintain both in theory and in practice. The theoretical distinction is based on the following analysis: With respect to a past act, a client who has done what may be a crime has the right to assistance of counsel in defending himself against prosecution arising from the act; counsel cannot defend the client effectively unless the client gives him all the facts, good and bad; the client will be inhibited from giving all the facts unless he is assured that the disclosure will not be used against him; therefore, the disclosure must be kept secret. On the other hand, a client whose act is only in contemplation

6. On the bar's interpretation of the 1974 amendment, see A.B.A. Committee on Professional Ethics, *Formal Opinion 341* (Sept. 30, 1975).

does not face the necessity of defending himself, and will do so only if he carries out his contemplated purpose; a course of action that if consummated will constitute a crime involves a serious and morally wrongful invasion of interests of others or of the community interest, which should be inhibited if possible; the threatened public injury or injury to others is not offset by any interest of the client; therefore, the incentive of secrecy need not and should not be provided to one who has revealed an intention to inflict such an injury.

This analysis is vulnerable to two objections. The objections move in opposite directions and indicate how uneasy a compromise has been reached in the formulation of the rule. On the one hand, it can be objected that information about future acts contemplated by the client should be as fully protected by secrecy as those concerning past conduct. The argument in support of this position would be as follows: A lawyer is not only an advocate in litigation but a counsellor about present troubles and future contingencies; there are circumstances in which violation of the law or intentionally deceiving another person may be morally justified or excusable and a client should be able to pursue his moral analysis informed by expert advice as to the legal aspects of his conduct; in addition, the chances that a lawyer as counsellor may dissuade his client from a wrongful purpose are at least as great as the chances that the consultation will reinforce the wrongful purpose, and opportunity for such dissuasion should be encouraged by giving it the protection of secrecy.

On the other hand, it could be said that even communications about a past crime or wrong should not be privileged. The analysis would be as follows: A person accused of wrongdoing has a right to demand that there be proof against him and, at least if the wrongdoing is a crime, a right to refrain from testifying and thus helping prove an accusation against himself. He has no right, however, to attack or discredit proofs against him unless he is willing to join in a search for "the whole truth," which would include revealing any admissions he might have made to anyone. The only purpose of consulting a lawyer is to get help in disconcerting others' proof, a course of action that is justified only if one is willing to open all proofs; admissions to one's lawyer are a kind of proof, like any other admission; therefore, what the client says to his lawyer should be open to disclosure.

It should quickly be noted that this last line of objection to attorney-client privilege enjoys no support in American law. Given our traditions about the relation between the citizen and the law, it probably never will. But as a moral and ethical proposition it has great strength: How can one who is under judgment ask for full and fair consideration of his cause and at the same time obstruct efforts to find out what that cause really is? To a laymen's eye, it is difficult to see the difference between burning incriminating files (or erasing tapes), both of which are improper by either a client or his lawyer, and suppressing what the lawyer has learned from or about the client. The effect of the suppression is to prevent the law from proceeding on the basis of the fullest available evidence and forces the legal process to place greater reliance on inference, conjecture, or suspicion, depending on what one calls it. That, a moralist might say, is a strange result if the aim is to base legal judgments on objective proof.

So much for the theoretical problems in trying to distinguish between past and future wrongs for purposes of defining the rule of confidentiality. What has been said hardly exhausts the subject. It is perhaps enough to show, however, that the rule of confidentiality when applied to crimes or frauds by the client rests on morally debatable grounds. The rules of the Code of Professional Responsibility may settle the debate for legal purposes but they surely cannot quiet the qualms of a conscientious lawyer who knows his client is swindling someone.

The distinction between past and future conduct is even more difficult to maintain in practical terms, at least for the modern business lawyer. The rules of confidentiality assume that all real modern instances fall into one of two stock situations. In the first situation, the client walks in, says to the lawyer that he is charged with murder, and then admits he shot the guy. Under the rules, that disclosure is confidential. In the other situation, the client walks in, discloses to the lawyer that he wants to kill the guy, and then goes out and does so. That disclosure is not confidential until the fatal shot is fired, although, as we have seen, the lawyer does not have to disclose it unless asked, which ordinarily he would not be until after the victim is already dead. The realities of modern business, on the other hand, bear little relation to this tidy dichotomy. They involve clients who "walked in" years ago and have since been continually provided with advice and assistance on all kinds of matters. They involve courses of client activity that originated years ago, continue in the present, and whose consequences will ramify into the more or less indefinite future. They also involve a complex web of legal rules governing the client, many of them carrying both penal sanctions and possibilities of ruinous civil liability and all of them ones which the client has both a duty to obey and incentives to avoid or violate.

To impose on such realities a distinction between past, present, and future is casuistical at best and often simply nonsense. Yet as the confidentiality rule now stands, the distinction is crucial. It is legally crucial because it determines whether the lawyer has the option, and perhaps the duty, to keep to himself that his client was, is, or will be cheating the government out of its taxes or little old ladies out of their savings. Beyond this technical question, the distinction is morally crucial. If the lawyer is not keeping silent on account of duty, what kind of person can he be to watch that kind of thing happen?

There is still a further aspect of the problem. The rule of confidentiality, wherever the lines are drawn that determine its scope, applies only to "clients." If the information in question was received from or concerns someone who is not a client, the secrecy rule has no application at all. Who is a "client"? As we shall see, that matter is far from simple, particularly for a lawyer to a corporation or government agency. But passing that question for the present, it should be remembered that lawyers find out a lot of "embarrassing or detrimental" things about people who are not their clients. For example, a lawyer may find that money to be paid his client is being obtained through fraud being practiced on a third person. He may find that money his client will pay to another person will not be reported by the latter as income for tax purposes. He may find that money his client is paying someone as a fee for services is really being used to bribe a public official, or that a person who has unsuccessfully tried to swindle his client has successfully swindled others.

In such circumstances, most lawyers keep silent, even if they have not merely suspicions but solid evidence of the wrongdoing by the nonclient. There are often impelling practical reasons for maintaining silence. If the crime or fraud is disclosed, the lawyer's client might be implicated as a joint or acquiescent wrongdoer. If a negotiation is pending between the lawyer's client and the wrongdoer, disclosure might upset a deal that the client needs, or frustrate a chance to get restitution to which the client is entitled. Furthermore, disclosure may mark the lawyer with his fellows as someone who tries not only to represent clients but to be a public police force as well, and hence not to be trusted when smelly matters have to be cleaned up. The problem of keeping silent about third-party wrongdoing therefore involves the question of what a lawyer may do for his client. This question is considered more fully below. But it is clear that one thing he can do, at least up to a point, is to keep dirty secrets not only of his clients but of others as well.

A third exception to the rule of confidentiality is one that must be galling to a layman. It is that the client's secrets may be revealed by the lawyer when doing so becomes necessary "to establish or collect his fee or to defend himself or his employees or associates against an accusation of wrongful conduct." The exception is of course designed to protect the lawyer against injustice at the hands of his client. If the confidentiality rule were applied when the lawyer sues to collect his fee, he could not prove what he did to earn it and thus could not prove his case. Similarly, if he is sued for malpractice or charged with misconduct in a disciplinary proceeding, and could not offer his own testimony about the transaction with the client, he might suffer unjust judgment.

This is perhaps fair enough as far as it goes. But of course the secret exchanges between the client and lawyer could also be relevant when the client refuses to pay someone other than his lawyer, or makes an accusation of wrongdoing against a third person. Suppose a person refused to pay his architect but admits to his lawyer that he ordered changes in the plans that he denies having ordered; or charges his accountant with having prepared a misleading financial statement but admits to his lawyer that he provided the misleading information on which the accountant relied. Why should the exception to the confidentiality rule not be at least so extended that a lawyer may testify to contradict a barefaced lie by his client? The lawyer now may do so when he is the target of a client's misrepresentation, the exception could be expanded to something like this: A lawyer may (must?) reveal secrets of his client when the client seeks to defend or prosecute a civil claim on the basis of facts contradicting evidence known to his lawyer. As we shall see when we get to the problem of

THE OFFICIAL RULES   33

prohibited assistance, the rule as it stands is only that the
lawyer may, perhaps must, withdraw from representing his
client in such circumstances; it does not permit him to reveal
his client's admissions, unless the claim concerns the lawyer
himself.

Conflict of Interest

The second basic principle governing the lawyer-client
relationship is that of loyalty. The principle is stated in the
ethical considerations part of the Code of Professional
Responsibility as follows: "Neither [a lawyer's] personal
interests, the interests of other clients, nor the desires of
third parties should be permitted to dilute his loyalty to his
client." This principle is given expression in a twofold scheme
of rules. First, there is a comprehensive prohibition against
a lawyer's acting for a client if his "professional judgment"
might be affected by his own interests or interests of other
clients that he represents. Second, there is a procedure for
lifting the prohibition by making "full disclosure" and obtaining the client's consent to the conflictual situation.
Alternatively, the lawyer may withdraw from representing
the client.

One kind of conflict between lawyer and client is that
arising out of transactions between them. The Code of
Professional Responsibility permits business transactions,
such as corporate ventures and real estate deals, between
lawyer and client. The rule is that if the two have "differing
interests therein" (whenever would they not?) and if the
lawyer is to act as the client's legal adviser "therein," the
lawyer may act as such so long as "the client has consented
after full disclosure." It might well be asked, if the lawyer
is permitted to be a legal adviser in such circumstances, why
his obligation should not be stated as follows: The lawyer

may act as legal adviser only if, in the subsequent course of the transaction, it can be shown that the client was served in the same way as he would have been served by a reasonably competent and protective lawyer who had no such conflict of interest. Among other things, this would make the legitimacy of the transaction turn not on what the lawyer said to the client (or said he said), but on what he actually did for him, which is what counts. Such a formulation of the rule, however, would leave the lawyer in a much more vulnerable position and thus would severly inhibit such transactions.

It might be noted that this kind of conflict of interest comes up infrequently for "elite" lawyers. They do not and will not get involved in business dealings with their clients except of two kinds: arrangements as to fee (or salary, in the case of lawyers directly employed by corporations) and serving as directors of corporations for which they or their partners were legal counsel. These problems are considered later on. The "business transactions" exception to the Code's conflict of interest rule, however, is very important to smaller firm and smaller city lawyers, who often take deferred compensation and pursue prospects for profit through a "piece of the action" in a client's business. Whether the rule permitting this kind of deal adequately protects clients is another question.

Another kind of conflict of interest can arise when the lawyer who serves a client is paid by someone else whose interests are not wholly compatible with those of the client. At one time, this was regarded as inherently bad. The maxims invoked were that "no man can serve two masters" (the context of which seems to have been forgotten) and "he who pays the piper calls the tune." If this position had been adhered to, it would have prohibited the arrangement whereby liability insurance companies pay for legal assistance to their insureds in suits brought for losses covered by the insurance.

Since that arrangement proved socially necessary, the old rule was relaxed. With the insurance company precedent firmly established, it is now the general rule that a lawyer may represent a client even though someone else is paying the cost, unless the funding source imposes constraints that prevent the lawyer from being loyal to the client. The fact remains that in such situations the lawyer has to cope with at least potential conflict. The following instances are illustrative:

— Representation of an insured by a lawyer employed by the insurance company (the problem being that the insured wants a big claim terminated within the limits of the policy, while the insurer wants to fight big claims even though there is risk of a judgment for more than the limits of the policy).
— Representation of a corporate officer by a lawyer employed by the corporation (the problem being that the corporation may be better off if it repudiates the action of the officer that is in question).
— Representation of a union member by a lawyer employed by the union (the interest of the member can conflict with that of his fellow members, for example if the question is seniority rights).
— Representation of a public official by government legal staff (we may recall Mr. St. Clair's interesting statement concerning Mr. Nixon that, being paid by the government, he represented "the Presidency", whatever that meant).
— Representation of black school children and their parents by an organization such as the N.A.A.C.P. (the organization wants bussing, but the parents may have different priorities).

These kinds of conflicts merge into a third type. This is the representation of two or more clients when the clients' interests conflict. As we noted in discussing the confidentiality rule, the Code's position is that the lawyer may represent both clients, but only if "he can adequately represent the interest of each and if each consents to the representation after full disclosure of the possible effect of such representation on the exercise of his independent professional judgment on behalf of each." This formulation is an improvement on the Code's treatment of conflicts between the lawyer and the client. It requires not only that there be "full disclosure" but also that the lawyer explain how the conflict might affect his representation (inviting the question why he shouldn't be required to do that when the conflict is between himself and the client). It also requires that, in some objective sense, he can be able "adequately" to represent both clients (again inviting the question why there should not be similar requirement when the conflict is between lawyer and client).

There are nevertheless some problems in this situation that the Code does not quite reach. One has been previously alluded to: How can the lawyer make "full disclosure" to each client without at the same time violating his duty to each of keeping their confidences confidential? Secondly, the rule openly acknowledges the situation to be one in which the lawyer's commitment to one client may inhibit the way in which he represents the other. This in turn implies two propositions: First, inhibited representation of a client is "adequate" under some circumstances; and second, when a lawyer is representing two or more clients whose interests conflict, he necessarily plays a somewhat different role than when he represents one of the clients and someone else represents the other.

Perhaps these implications do not follow. It can be said that if the conflict between the clients is such that the lawyer's representation of either may be inhibited in any way, then the conflict necessarily is one that precludes the lawyer from representing both. And it can be said that there is a single concept of the lawyer-client relationship: you have it or you do not. But this is to deny what seems obvious once it is conceded that a lawyer can serve two clients whose interests conflict, that is, that he has to handle the situation differently than if they did not conflict. And if this is accepted, there are several other permissible implications.

First, there is no unitary concept of the attorney-client relationship. If a lawyer could have one set of responsibilities when acting protectively for one person and another when acting protectively for more than one person, he could have one set when representing a client in a trial and another when conducting settlement negotiations; one set when an advocate, another when an office counsellor and planner; one set when a wholly passive counsellor, another when called on to take action in behalf of a client. Differences in these responsibilities may allow a lawyer to act for two or more persons in one context but not in another. Thus, what constitutes "loyalty" to the client may depend on what mission is being undertaken for him.

Similarly, there is no unitary concept of a client. A "client" may be one whose interest is the lawyer's exclusive concern, or one whose interest is among several for which the lawyer must be concerned. Thus, one can be under a lawyer's protection without being a "full fledged" client, that is, one whom the lawyer must protect to the exclusion of everyone else. But if the lawyer's duty to a client is modified by his duty to another client, it also is modified by duties to people who are not his clients. Would an ethical lawyer carry out a swindle on a third party just because his client wants him to? He would not, and his reason would be that he has duties to third persons that he will not violate even at the behest of a client. That such obligations to others exist—and, indeed, that there are all kinds of such obligations—means that the duties to a particular client can be precisely stated only with recognition of those other obligations, and therefore vary from one context to another. Hence, the duty to client, far from being absolute as the Code suggests, is relative like all other duties. To the extent that the rhetoric of the Code suggests otherwise, it is misleadingly simplistic.

Prohibited Assistance

A lawyer has powerful weapons to use on behalf of a client. He can bring a lawsuit, knowing that his accusations are absolutely privileged under the law of libel and that his client cannot be charged with the opposing party's costs of defense except in certain special circumstances. If he brings the suit, within wide limits he can make it expensive, protracted, acrimonious, and a vehicle for invading the opposing party's time and peace of mind. He can threaten suit. In negotiations that he wants to bring to quick conclusion, he can be aggressive, peremptory, and overbearing, or accommodating, compliant, and seductive. In negotiations that he does not want to bring to quick conclusion, he can be grasping, inflexible, hypertechnical, and dilatory, or evasive, distracted, and unreachable on the telephone. In litigation brought against his client, he can make it expensive, protracted, etc., also without subjecting his client to liability for the plaintiff's expenses, and often complicate it further with counterclaims, new issues and parties, or by starting new litigation in another court. If the matter involves a government agency and he wants expedition, sometimes he can get it; if he doesn't want the matter to move, he can be hypertechnical, etc., and perhaps succeed in enlarging the issues into ones of "public interest" that can be considered to death. In all these endeavors the lawyer himself is for all practical purposes legally immune.

The lawyer has still other weaponry. He can write contracts that are onerous, promote legislation that creates discriminatory preferences, and fashion all manner of arrangements that literally comply with law but avoid its intended effects. He can give his client an informed opinion about the discount rate on law enforcement, from which the client can deduce the risk that a particular course of action will be detected or questioned. Within limits he can reconstruct reality by portrayal of facts. He can also suggest what kinds of misrepresentations might be advantageous for the client to make, and help him make them. And he can lie, steal, fabricate or destroy evidence, and help with coverups. There are clients who at one time or another would like all of these services. All except the last mentioned are legal and are permitted by the Disciplinary Rules.

The forms of prohibited assistance fall into two principal categories, those in general and those specifically concerning litigation. The general prohibitions are that a lawyer may not:

— Take action whose purpose is "merely to harass or maliciously injure another." Action that has some other purpose as well is not impermissible.
— Conceal anything "he is required by law to reveal."
— "Make a false statement of law or fact."
— Fabricate evidence. (There is no express prohibition on destroying evidence. The penal law prohibits destruction of evidence, although it applies only when an enforcement action is under way or in prospect.)
— "Counsel or assist his client in conduct that the lawyer knows to be illegal or fraudulent."
— Permit the client to conceal a fraud that the lawyer has learned about, unless he learned about it through a "privileged communication."

The prohibitions specifically concerning litigation are that a lawyer may not:

— Advance a claim or defense that cannot be supported by "good faith argument."

- "Threaten to present criminal charges solely to obtain advantage in a civil matter."
- Disregard the rules of procedure or rulings of the court made in the course of litigation.
- Fail to apprise the court of "directly adverse" applicable legal authority if the opposing party has failed to bring it to the court's attention.
- Assert any proposition that he has no reason to believe is supportable by proof.
- Ask plainly irrelevant questions or questions whose only purpose is to degrade a witness or other person.
- Assert his personal belief as to facts that are in dispute.[7]

These injunctions can be summarized in somewhat different terms. First, if a lawyer makes a statement about something, he should not lie. Second, he should not assist his client in doing something that is illegal or fraudulent. Third, he should not pervert litigation by advancing baseless contentions. Given the range of relationships in which a lawyer may find himself and the range of functions he can perform, these injunctions are remarkably narrow in scope. Indeed, on more careful examination they are even narrower than they first appear.

For one thing, most of the prohibitions relate to conduct of litigation. This focus may betray a preoccupation with lawyer misbehavior that affects other lawyers, for the Code contemplates an adversary system of litigation and in the adversary system there is always a lawyer on the other side. But because there is a lawyer on the other side, the chances that misconduct in litigation will be undetected and unremedied are almost certainly more remote than in other

7. In addition to the Code of Professional Responsibility's provisions on advocacy, a somewhat different set of rules has been formulated by the American College of Trial Lawyers in that group's *Code of Trial Conduct* (1972).

circumstances. Furthermore, a lawyer's misconduct in litigation carries with it the risk of his losing credit and credibility with the court before which it occurred, and the maintenance of credit is of vital professional concern to most lawyers who appear in court very often. Thus, proscribing misconduct in litigation as professionally unethical has relatively little independent practical significance.

This is even more readily apparent if the Code's definition of litigation misconduct is brought into focus. In effect, what is proscribed are acts of litigation that are fraudulent, that is, which are without any basis whatever. A different standard could be established, for example that a contention should not be advanced unless a reasonably fair-minded lawyer would think it has a substantial chance of being sustained. This poses a more general question concerning the ethics of the adversary system, which will be considered later.

The other two basic injunctions are also narrower than they might seem. The rule that a lawyer must not lie applies only if he is called upon to say something, and then applies only to what he says. He ordinarily has no obligation to correct a misapprehension or to tell "the whole truth" when he speaks to a subject.[8] Hence, the lawyer's duty to tell the truth has little or no greater breadth than that imposed upon him under the law of fraud. Furthermore, we have seen that a lawyer has broad responsibilities for preserving confidences, both of his clients and of others. The injunction against saying untruths is therefore always qualified by an even more powerful injunction against saying anything at all.

Finally, the prohibition against assisting a client in doing something that is illegal or fraudulent means a lot less than it

---

8. For a well-developed argument that there should be a duty to correct misapprehension, see Rubin, "A Causerie on Lawyers' Ethics in Negotiation," 35 *La. L. Rev.* 577 (1975).

might seem to. In the first place, there is no prohibition on defending a client against charges arising from past conduct; being ready to defend such conduct is not regarded as assisting it. In the second place, the American Bar Association Committee on Professional Ethics has interpreted a related rule, requiring that a lawyer reveal a client's fraud once he has learned of it, to mean that a lawyer may not intercept client fraud if doing so requires disclosure of facts that might embarrass the client, which exhausts most real life possibilities. Third, although the Code says otherwise, many lawyers believe it is not unethical to put a client on the witness stand knowing that he is going to lie. Their theory is that the refusal to lead the client to such testimony would be a tipoff that the client intends to perjure himself, and therefore would be a betrayal of the client.

In summary, close analysis of the Disciplinary Rules of the Code of Professional Responsibility indicates that, so far as the problem of confidentiality is concerned, they make preservation of a client's secrets a value preferred over everything except interdicting crimes of violence; so far as conflict of interest is concerned, they recognize the problem but say very little about how it should be resolved; and so far as prohibited assistance is concerned, their effect is little more than to make unethical what is in any event a violation of law or professionally stupid.

The lawyer who believes his professional conduct should be more fully enlightened must therefore look elsewhere. In searching for other norms, however, he acts under the injunction that he "should represent a client zealously within the bounds of the law." Thus he must be mindful that measures not prohibited in aid of a client are approximately obligatory, for failure to use them is a failure of "zeal." If there remains an ethically autonomous course for the conscientious lawyer, it lies between Scylla and Charybdis.

3. Who Is the Client?

The lawyer's professional responsibilities may not end with concern for his client, but clearly they start there. Confidential information is a secret if it relates to a client, valuable evidence if it relates to someone else. Conflict with the client must be avoided, conflict with everyone else is what a lawyer is retained to handle. How far a lawyer is prepared to go in partisan aggressiveness is the measure of what he will do, at the same time, for a client and to other people. Identifying the client is thus critical in the lawyer's orientation to "relevant others" and in their orientation to him.

In the traditional lore of the legal profession, identifying the client is not a problem. The client is the troubled fellow who walks into the office, papers in hand, wanting someone to help him in a legal matter. If all real world lawyer-client relationships began this way and involved nothing else, the question of client identity would always be answered before the relationship begins.

For the lawyer retained by an organization such as a corporation or government agency, identifying the client is much more complicated.[1] Client identity is ambiguous, continuously problematic, and requires resolution by

1. See Donnell, *The Corporate Counsel—A Role Study* (1970); Pierce, "The Code of Professional Responsibility in the Corporate World," 6 *Mich. J. L. Reform* 350 (1973). On the lawyer for the government agency, see Dam, "The Special Responsibility of Lawyers in the Executive Branch," 55 *Chicago Bar Record* 4 (1974); Poirer, "The Federal Government Lawyer and Professional Ethics," 60 *A.B.A.J.* 1541 (1974).

conscious choice. The discussion that follows centers on this question. But it is worth noting that the question also confronts the "ordinary" legal practitioner. Take some instances:

— A lawyer for a partnership contemplates a venture that has both the prospect of great profit and the risk of heavy liability; one of the partners has large personal assets that would be chargeable with losses, the other has entrepreneurial skills that can exploit the opportunity; the lawyer for the partnership is asked whether a separate limited partnership or corporation should be set up for a new venture, aware of the fact that if the wealthy partner's personal credit is not put on the line the banks may not lend the necessary capital.
— A lawyer who has drafted a will for a husband and wife and handled business transactions for the husband is consulted by the husband about a separation of the marriage, aware that a conflict could arise concerning the property settlement and child custody.
— A lawyer who has served an aging and wealthy person in handling her property is consulted by her children who say that she is becoming senile and perhaps should have a guardianship established.
— A lawyer for a school district is consulted by a member of the schoolboard who believes another member has undisclosed interests in certain contracts the school district has entered into.
— A lawyer is asked by the wife of a man in jail to represent him in a prosecution for having beaten their child into insensibility.
— A lawyer is retained by parents of a child to represent the child in juvenile court on a charge that the child has told the parents is false but which he admits to the lawyer is true.

WHO IS THE CLIENT?

The lawyer's initial problem in all these situations is to determine who the client is. The legal profession's rules of ethics provide what is perhaps worse than no guidance. Instead of saying how or on what grounds the question of client identity is to be resolved, they assume it has somehow been resolved *ex ante*. From that point they tell the lawyer that whomever he considers his client should be embraced and whomever he considers his nonclient should be placed at arm's length. But in the real world, as the illustrations given suggest, the identity of the client may not be established until after some critical decisions have to be made, and may never be unambigiously established at all.

An equally serious question associated with the question of client identity is: "What do I do about the nonclient?" In every situation in which the identity of the client is in question, there is another person present to whom the lawyer has some kind of tie—the partner, the spouse, the child or parent, the fellow school board member in the illustrations mentioned. The lawyer has a responsibility of some kind to that person, perhaps as his attorney but at any rate one that, at least morally, is greater than that which he owes to other people generally. The rules, however, contemplate that there are only two kinds of "relevant others"—clients and nonclients. They do not consider the possibility that there are people who might be called "quasi-clients," people to whom the lawyer owes a duty greater than that due strangers but secondary to that due to the client.

The problem of client identity is compounded when the persons confronting the lawyer are uncertain about the stance they want to take in the situation before them. Thus, if a spouse clearly wants a divorce, the lawyer can orient himself to both spouses much more definitely than if, as is often the case, the spouse to whom he is talking is unsure of his or her feelings and objectives. So also, if one school board member is plainly antipathetic to a colleague whom he suspects of misconduct, the lawyer can orient himself to his role problem more definitely than if the member has suggested that "maybe this thing needs looking into." When the prospective primary client is uncertain how to define his own relationship to the other person in the transaction, the lawyer's position is inevitably tentative and ambiguous. This mood is quite the opposite of that in the Code's projection, in which there is a person who is a "client" in a face-off with a person who is not. It may be speculated that the positioning envisioned by the Code is one that lawyers wish existed at initial contact and into which they may seek to transform the situation as soon as possible. This would explain why lawyers sometimes turn a squabble into a fight: It clarifies the lawyer's own role, extricating him from a situation in which otherwise everyone eventually may turn on him and none pay for his trouble.

In different form, similar problems continually confront the lawyer for a large organization. It is a problem that the Code of Responsibility simply evades. The Code says:

A lawyer employed or retained by a corporation or similar entity owes his allegiance to the entity and not to a stockholder, director, officer, employee, representative, or other person connected with the entity.

The counterpart rule for government lawyers says it is the government that is the client. When the legal matter in question is between the organization and an outsider, these propositions are truisms—of course the client is the organization. When the legal matter poses a question within the corporation or the government, however, the "entity" referent provides no help. The unanswered question for the lawyer is: What individual should I treat as representing the organization so I can know whom to represent? Or, conversely: Whom should I decide to represent so I can know what individual to treat as the organization?

This is a critical point of departure for the lawyer to an organization. All the Seven Springs lawyers experienced it.

WHO IS THE CLIENT?

It can begin with the following encounter: "The executive vice-president comes into your office unannounced or having said only that he needs to talk to you right away. His voice has told you something is wrong. He closes the door, tensely sits down, and then starts to speak, haltingly and in obvious distress. He says that _____." The blank is filled with the following kinds of things:

— A report certified to the government as correct is actually false and the empolyees who submitted it probably knew it was false."
— "The sales division has been following marketing arrangements that legal counsel has warned would probably violate the antitrust laws."
— "A dangerous defect in one of the company's products, the subject of a pending suit by an injured customer, probably exists in a whole product run, although the production manager had testified otherwise in his pretrial testimony."
— "Certain expense account claims by the chairman of the board are false and represent not only money he shouldn't have received but money he probably failed to report as personal income."
— "The vice president for international sales approved payoffs that were illegal in the country where made and which have been improperly included as expense deductions in the corporation's U.S. income tax return."

Appreciating the lawyer's dilemma in such situations requires some explication of the legal relationships inside a corporation. There are two basic conceptions of a corporation. In formal legal conception, the stockholders own the company. Creditors such as suppliers, employees, and bondholders have payment claims against it. The board of directors superintends the corporation for the benefit of the stockholders, with deference to the claims of creditors. The officers manage the operation, under the supervision of the directors. A different conception of the corporation is expressed in the modern "realist" view. In the "realist" conception of a corporation, the officers run the company; the directors more or less passively scrutinize the officers' management and ratify its managerial decisions; the loan creditors exercise financial control on the risks that management takes, depending on the company's debt structure; and the stockholders get some combination of dividends and appreciation of their investment. Both conceptions are valid. The "realist" conception is substantially correct as applied to most large corporations under normal operating conditions, but the formal conception defines legal responsibilities that become critical if the corporation gets into financial or legal difficulties.[2]

Corporate financial or legal crises of the kind described above, when they occur, are directly the result of action or inaction by the corporation's officers and other employees working under their direction. Legal liability for the consequences begins with them, for the officers sometimes can be held personally liable to the corporation for getting it into trouble and may also be liable to outsiders, such as the government or creditors. If the derelictions are ones that the board of directors knew about, or should have known about if they had fulfilled their supervisory responsibility, the directors may be personally liable to the stockholders and to

---

2. For a collection of relevant organization theory literature and one approach to some of the legal problems involved, see Note, "Decision-making Models and the Control of Corporate Crime," 85 *Yale L. J.* 1091 (1976). For a careful legal analysis, see Eisenberg, "Legal Models of Management Structure in the Modern Corporation," 63 *Calif. L. Rev.* 375 (1975). For still more references and a strong viewpoint, see Stone, *Where the Law Ends: The Social Control of Corporate Behavior* (1975).

outsiders. The corporation itself is liable to third persons injured by the misconduct, such as victims of antitrust violations, but the existence and extent of its liability can depend on whether the conduct in question was "unauthorized," that is, violative of company policy. All these forms of potential liability increase if the conduct is persisted in and may take on an additional intentional quality if persisted in after counsel has appraised them to be wrongful. Furthermore, they may occasion not only damages liability but also criminal penalties and such sanctions as loss of license (for licensed industries) and delistment as an eligible contractor (for companies doing business with government agencies).

When a legal problem of this sort comes to the attention of the lawyer for the corporation, he has two issues to contend with. The first is how he should conduct himself apart from the question of client identity. That is, he must decide whether the situation involves a "past" wrong, so that he must treat its disclosure as confidential, or a wrong continuing into the future, in which event the rule of confidentiality may not apply, particularly if the conduct may be a crime. This problem of classification, which has already been considered, is difficult in itself, owing to the often illusory character of the distinction between past and future.

Beyond this, the lawyer has to deal with the problem of identifying his client. The problem is difficult both morally and legally. The question has a moral aspect because the lawyer is faced with subordinating and perhaps seriously injuring the interest of a person who has trusted him in the past. In a family setting, the relationship between the lawyer and the person before him—perhaps he can be called a "heretofore client"—can have been intertwined with long personal friendship. In the corporate setting, the individual can have been a business friend of long standing. When the heretofore client begins unburdening himself, he is only doing what the lawyer has encouraged him to do in the past.

If the lawyer refuses to listen, he must appear to be violating a trusting relationship and to be abandoning a friendship. On the other hand, if the lawyer does listen, he can hear things that implicate not only the heretofore client but the organization that both of them are being paid to serve. And if the lawyer listens, he knows that the person before him supposes that the disclosure is confidential. If the lawyer is not certain that he can keep the disclosure confidential, his listening to it is the first step of what can turn out to be a betrayal of a confidence, and therefore a grave moral wrong.

In terms of the lawyer's legal obligations, the situation is equally complex.[3] When the corporate officer begins talking, the lawyer must be mindful that a lawyer-client relationship is in the making. At this point, if the lawyer treats the corporate officer as the client, and if he learns things that may subject the officer to criminal or civil liability, the lawyer is bound by the rule of confidentiality not to disclose the matters to others, for example to the board of directors. But the lawyer's general retainer, if we may call it that, is to the corporation. The board will consider that it "is" the corporate client, and expect the lawyer eventually to advise the board what to do, including advice about the possibility of proceeding against the executive. The lawyer may find himself unable to do that without violating his professional duty to the executive. The board will then feel at least disappointed and very likely betrayed.

On the other hand, if the lawyer treats the executive as a nonclient, he must consider giving him some sort of "Miranda warning," that is, tell him that any disclosures he makes may have to be revealed to the board and perhaps to others. Giving a "Miranda warning" represents a decision by the lawyer that his client is the board of directors and not the

---

3. See also Barnett and McDonald, "What the CEO [Chief Executive Officer] Should Expect from His General Counsel," in Glover and Simon, *The Chief Executive's Handbook* at 899 (1976).

officer. If such a warning is given, the lawyer will leave the executive in the lurch, perhaps requiring him to go elsewhere for legal advice and therewith drawing some kind of line between himself and the company he has been bound to serve.

In taking that step, the lawyer in effect issues an interlocutory decree of divorce between the executive and the board, on no authority but the lawyer's own. The decree is necessarily based on inadequate information, for the warning immediately inhibits complete disclosure of what the situation is all about. If in the fullness of time the board decides to stand behind the officer, the subsequent relationship between the lawyer and the client can be awkward, to say the least. Even if the lawyer proves right in his decision, the warning, having impaired the lawyer's ability to find out all the facts, will make it more difficult for him to advise the corporate client how to proceed in its best interests. The warning probably also will have triggered a demoralizing division within the corporation's management, with consequent impairment of its efficiency. The contretemps may stimulate a spate of rumors and leaks that make impossible maintaining confidentiality between the lawyer and the board, which now "is" the client.

There is another legal aspect of the "Miranda warning" that may have far-reaching consequences. To give the warning is to treat the executive as a nonclient. Information received from a nonclient can be a "secret" of the corporate client that the lawyer should not disclose except to those who personate the client, that is, the board of directors. But such information is not a communication *from* a client, for the executive is not the client. The disclosure is not covered by the attorney-client privilege, as it would be if the executive is treated as the client. Hence, whatever the lawyer hears from the executive after having given the "Miranda warning" is information that a court may compel him to reveal, even though it may be very damaging to the corporation. Giving the "Miranda warning" is necessary to protect the executive but it also reduces the protection given the corporation under the attorney-client privilege. Thus, whichever way the lawyer decides who is his "client," he creates potentially serious consequences for someone who up to that point had regarded him as a confidential adviser.

The next stage remove is the board of directors. Until it has received the bad news, the board most likely will have been highly supportive of—or perhaps dominated by—the officers whose conduct is immediately in question. The board may well be unreceptive to the lawyer's message unless it is solidly documented, but documentation may be lacking. If the lawyer does not disclose to the board what he knows, and the board "is" the corporation, then he is holding out on his client. If he does disclose, he may have betrayed what the executive thought was a confidence. Furthermore, when he takes the matter to the board he implicates the board members in the problem, because their responsibility and potential legal liability is affected by the extent of their knowledge. If they then take appropriate remedial action, their very action can alert potential adversaries of something afoot that may be the basis of legal action against the corporation. If they do not act, they may be regarded as having violated their duties to the stockholders and perhaps have become accomplices so far as concerns liability to outsiders. And so the lawyer may have to consider the stockholders as the "client."[4]

At this stage of remove, the circles of risk and duty are still further enlarged. Again the lawyer has to face the problems of acting on limited information and jeopardizing his personal and professional honor. Furthermore, at this

---

4. See O'Neal and Thompson, "Vulnerability of Professional-Client Privilege in Shareholder Litigation," 31 *Bus. Lawyer* 1775 (1976).

WHO IS THE CLIENT?

stage if not before, maintaining confidentiality within the corporation becomes a practical impossibility, whoever may be regarded as the client. There is no way in which the stockholders of a widely held corporation can be advised of potential legal liability without at the same time putting the matter in the public domain.

This, then, is the web of risks and obligations that is agitated when the identity of the client is in question. The terms in which the Seven Springs participants discussed this problem are themselves interesting. Their sense of duty was strong, which means the question of direction of duty was correlatively more dilemmatic. Their personal attachment to the company people they worked with was also strong, belying the frosty image of the corporate lawyer. Duty and attachment were thus in conflict: "You try to be a decent human being"; "You don't rat on a person if you can avoid it." The lawyers knew their own conduct could be subject to scrutiny: "You have to keep your partners in mind"; "The auditors have their job, too"; "You're not going to be part of a coverup." They recognized a transcending if vaguely conceived constituency beyond the immediate corporate incumbents: "The corporation has a duty to the public"; "there is such a thing as corporate citizenship." They knew their self-interest was involved, for their reputation for professional skillfulness, their personal honor, and their future incomes were at risk.

The dramatic scenario is not reenacted every day. But in more subtle form it is the stuff of law practice. The company's product line cannot be made perfect for consumers; how far should the company go, how far should its lawyers suggest that it go, in establishing inspection procedures to assure the products are safe? The company's controls on factory pollution cannot be made perfect; how far should it go to safeguard the health of employees and denizens of "the environment?" A company's tax reporting can be unexceptional only if it resolves every doubtful issue in favor of the government; what should be the threshhold for reporting transactions that are ambiguous under the tax law? There is no such thing as "full disclosure" in marketing securities; how far should a corporation go in making disclosure, particularly when dissemination of the information can affect its competitive position?

These are tough legal questions quite apart from the problem of client identity. Each such question has to be resolved not only by the corporation as an "entity" but, at least in the first instance, by the decision of some specific officer or employee. His decision has implications not only for the corporation as an entity but for the officer or employee himself, and that leads back to the question of identifying the client.

The same kind of problem confronts the government lawyer. Only in relatively few situations is there a possibility that a course of action by an official will result in civil or criminal liability, occasioning a reproduction of the Watergate drama. Watergate reminds us, however, that this can happen at any level of government. Some types of officials, the police for example, risk such liability more or less as a matter of course in their work. The problem also arises whenever an agency is investigated by Congress, the General Accounting Office, or the F.B.I. How does the agency lawyer orient himself to the officials who are under investigation? In tamer form, the problem arises whenever there is a policy conflict having legal dimensions (when does it not?) between agencies or between levels or divisions within an agency. For here, as in the large corporation with its own staff of attorneys, lawyers are assigned to specific departments and divisions, providing legal advice to particular individual officials. At the same time, their employment as professionals is by "the government."

Several different approaches to the problem of client

identity can be imagined. One is to say that the concept of corporate entity should disappear once a potential conflict has emerged among the individuals associated with the entity. This means, however, that the lawyer is responsible to everyone or to no one. Another is to say that the lawyer has to elect among the individuals at the outset and declare that others will have to get their own counsel. Even assuming that the entity is willing to pay the lawyers' fees on these terms, or that the individuals involved can afford to do so if the company is not, this results in there having to be "a lawyer for everybody." The Seven Springs participants recorded the anger and exasperation that this idea engendered in corporate managers, who thought the whole business was simultaneously a cop out for the lawyers and a way of running up legal fees. Apart from expense, this approach is also often impractical. Whatever course of action is ultimately adopted for the corporation, ordinarily it can most intelligently and effectively be carried out only with the assistance of the corporation's regular lawyers. Outside counsel may not be able to be deployed quickly enough to avoid serious damage to the company's interest. Even when outside counsel is brought in, they will seek briefing from the lawyers already on hand, and this raises once more the question of client identity. Hence, the lawyer who is under retainer to the corporation usually cannot escape having to decide who is the client and who is only the heretofore client.

Still another approach is to say that the rule of confidentiality, which is what makes critical the problem of client identification, ought never to apply to entities such as corporations or government agencies. Such an approach would take one long step further in the direction of "government in the sunshine," for private entities as well as government itself. This approach has been seriously espoused and is not easily met. It is easy to understand why it is thought that the important decisions of corporations and government agencies should not be shrouded in secrecy. And yet there are competing considerations. As a political matter, it would not be easy to withdraw the privilege from large corporations and governments but retain it for small corporations, businessmen, tax avoiders, and criminals; indeed, in a referendum the group least likely to be awarded the privilege might well be the criminally accused. More fundamentally, the decisions of corporations and of government often involve unpleasant matters that are difficult to face squarely even in confidence: the incompetence, inattentiveness, cowardice, disloyalty, greed, ambition, and deviousness of superiors, subordinates, friends, foes, allies, opposite numbers, supposedly disinterested third persons such as judges and other officials, and the client himself. Without confidentiality, such matters can be spoken of only in code or by indirection, which gives the subtle-minded an enormous advantage over the straightforward in the decision-making process. It thus has to be considered that the rule of confidentiality, by allowing occasions of definite secrecy, promotes openness as a normal social style. At all events, as things now stand the lawyer takes the rule of confidentiality as a given and has to decide who his client is. Under the rules, that person's affairs are something the lawyer can pursue but not reveal.

This approach, however, simply does not recognize the ambivalence of the lawyer's position in relation to his clients. There are and clearly should be legal limits on what a lawyer may do for a client. He should not be allowed to help the client kill, steal, or lie to someone who has a right to expect the truth. These duties imply correlative duties to people who are not the lawyer's clients. Once this much is accepted, the question is not whether a lawyer owes a duty "to" his client and not "to" others, but how he should shape his courses of action given that he has duties to both his clients and others. This implies that a lawyer's course of action might vary according to the character of his relationship with others, whether "clients" or not, and that the responsibilities he might assume could vary as events unfold. It thus implies that the concept of a "client" is not a premise but a conclusion, and one admitting of various inferences as to how the lawyer should comport himself.

Since the profession's rules of ethics do not conceive of this possibility, they do not offer guidance as to what alternative courses of action might be appropriate under various circumstances. It is difficult to imagine a set of prescriptions that could definitively offer such guidance, any more than definitive prescriptions can be supplied for resolving the moral dilemmas of everyday life. If that is so, the lawyer has to let his judgment, perhaps one might say his conscience, be his guide. This is to say, however, that he is inevitably a moral actor in his professional work. He must make choices on his own and cannot lay off the responsibility for them on "duty to client."

This is about where the Seven Springs participants came out.

4. Lawyer for the Situation

The problem of deciding who is the client arises when a lawyer supposes that a conflict of interest prevents him from acting for all the people involved in a situation. That is, if the interests of the potential clients were in harmony, or could be harmonized, no choice would have to be made between them and the lawyer could act for all. When the lawyer feels that he can act for all, it can be said simply that he has several clients at the same time. When the clients are all involved in a single transaction, however, the lawyer's responsibility is rather different from what it is when he represents several clients in transactions that have nothing to do with each other. This difference is suggested by the proposition that a lawyer serving more then one client in a single transaction represents "the situation."

The term is the invention of Louis D. Brandeis, Justice of the United States Supreme Court and before that practitioner of law in Boston. It emerged in a hearing in which Brandeis's professional ethics as a lawyer had been questioned.[1]

Brandeis seems to have been the only first class American lawyer whose professional ethics have been the subject of a formal investigation. The occasion was the 1916 Senate hearings on his nomination as Justice of the Supreme Court. Brandeis's nomination to the Court by President Wilson was bitterly opposed, chiefly by the conservative establishment within the legal profession. The opposition appears actually to have been based on the fact that Brandeis was an intel-

---

1. For an account of the Brandeis case, see Frank, "The Legal Ethics of Louis D. Brandeis," 17 *Stan. L. Rev.* 683 (1965).

lectually powerful liberal and a Jew, but ostensibly it was based on alleged improprieties in his professional conduct. One charge, which did not hold up, was that Brandeis represented some clients too resolutely. The other charge was that his representation of some clients was not resolute enough in that he had simultaneously acted for clients who had conflicts of interest. The attack ultimately failed, but out of it came the notion of "lawyer for the situation."

The Brandeis case is unusual because it involved the realities of a good lawyer's professional relationship with his clients. Most other formal examinations of lawyers' professional conduct fall into two categories. The first includes disciplinary proceedings in which a lawyer is charged with misconduct thought to warrant disbarment, suspension or reprimand. Statistically there are relatively few such cases, no more than about 150 a year across the country actually going to conclusion. Few if any involve the kinds of problems that a competent lawyer is really concerned about in his own practice. Rather, the disciplinary cases typically involve unfair professional competition (advertising, ambulance chasing, etc.), criminal misconduct (typically tax evasion), gross incompetence (failing to file a lawsuit on time, for example), or purloining clients' funds. The decided cases in this category are interesting chiefly for the fact that the sanctions imposed often seem mild, which says something about the effectiveness of a disciplinary apparatus as a means of inducing conformity to rules of professional conduct. The cases may also give prominence to gross violations of the rules of professional conduct and thus obscure the more subtle ethical problems encountered by most practitioners. They are essentially a police court jurisprudence.

The other context in which lawyers' professional conduct is examined is in bar association advisory opinions on questions of ethics. These are quasi-official. They do not have the force of law but they are at least admonitory and they contribute to the profession's definition of itself. An advisory opinion is issued upon a stated set of facts presented by someone, usually a lawyer, wishing to have the bar's official view of an ethical question. The facts are almost always stated *ex parte*, either by a lawyer seeking to justify himself or by a critical colleague seeking to have him anathemized. The fact statements are also almost always given in relatively abstract terms, partly because giving full details would risk disclosure of a client's affairs or liability for professional libel. The opinions are correspondingly abstract and often dogmatic, being clean-cut answers to hypothetical problems but providing less illumination for the messy ethical questions of real life. It might be added that, considered as a whole, they betray serious inconsistency on such critical questions as a lawyer's obligation to intercept a client's perpetration of fraud.

The Brandeis hearing was different. No one accused Brandeis of offenses such as theft or tax evasion, or of breaching the etiquette of professional competition. The facts in the questioned transactions were developed bilaterally, by Brandeis's supporters on the one hand and his opponents on the other, and in substantially complete complexity. What emerged was a portrayal of real life law practice.

The transactions complained of included the following: First, Brandeis had at one time represented one party in a transaction, later represented someone else in a way that impinged on that transaction. Second, he had acted in situations where those he served had conflicting interests, for example by putting together the bargain between parties to a business deal. Third, he had acted for a family business and continued so to act after a falling out among the family required reorganization of the business arrangement. Fourth, over a course of several years he had mediated and adjusted interests of the owners and creditors of a business in such a way as to keep the business from foundering.

LAWYER FOR THE SITUATION

The objections to Brandeis's conduct in all these situations were twofold. One was that his conduct was unethical per se because he represented conflicting interests. The other was that he had not adequately made clear to the clients that their interests were in conflict. On the second point, Brandeis acknowledged that at least in some instances he may not have adequately explained the situation to the clients and adequately defined his role as he saw it. Having acknowledged this, he defended his conduct not only on the ground of its being common practice but also on the ground that it was right. In instances questioned, he said, he did not regard himself as being lawyer for one of the parties to the exclusion of the others, but as "lawyer for the situation." Eventually, the charge did not so much collapse as become submerged in concessions from other reputable lawyers that they had often done exactly as Brandeis.

Brandeis's term was mentioned by the Seven Springs participants as descriptive of many settings in which they had found themselves, among them:

— Acting for a partnership or corporation, not only as legal adviser but also as mediator, go-between, and balance wheel among the principals in the business.
— Acting as an informal trustee for second and third generation members of a family having various active and passive interests in inherited property holdings.
— Acting as counsel, board member, and business affairs advisor for charitable organizations such as hospitals, libraries, and foundations.
— Acting as intermediary between a business and its creditors in a period of financial difficulties.
— Acting as intermediary between a corporate chief executive and his board of directors in the face of fundamental differences of policy.
— Acting as something like a marriage broker between clients

wanting to settle a complex contract arrangement on terms that would be "fair to everyone."

Similar functions are performed by lawyers on corporate legal staffs regarding differences between divisions and levels in the corporation, and by lawyers for government agencies that become enmeshed in conflicts of policy. It is safe to say that "ordinary" practitioners do the same sorts of things all the time for small businesses, families, public bodies such as school boards, and local civic and political organizations.

The Code of Professional Responsibility recognizes only a fragment of this kind of lawyering, and with some reluctance at that. It observes that a lawyer may "serve as an impartial arbitrator or mediator" between clients. It is not clear what this is supposed to mean. It may mean "impartial arbitrator" as one thing and "mediator" as another; it may mean "impartial arbitrator" and "impartial mediator." Although the difference in interpretation may be only a quibble, more is involved than may be at first apparent.

The term "impartial arbitrator" refers to a quite definite legal function, in which one person acts as a judge and decides a legal controversy that has broken out between two other persons. The term "impartial mediator" is approximately as definite, and means a person who assumes a role of neutral go-between in a dispute that the parties are trying to resolve by negotiation. Both roles presuppose the existence of a ripened dispute. They also presuppose that each party is speaking for himself, with the third person hearing both and responding accordingly. If this is what the Code is referring to, it falls far short of what Brandeis had in mind and far short also of the situations described by the Seven Springs lawyers.

On the other hand, if the Code means to say "mediator," as well as "impartial arbitrator," a much broader connotation

LAWYER FOR THE SITUATION

might be suggested. It can imply a role in which the lawyer becomes involved when the difference between the parties is still only a future contigency. It can imply that the lawyer is a spokesman for the position of each of the parties, as well as one who listens to the parties express their positions for themselves. It can imply that the lawyer is actively involved, indeed aggressively involved, in exploring alternative arrangements by which the positions of the parties can be accommodated in a comprehensive resolution of the matter at hand.

Lawyers do indeed find themselves in the roles contemplated by the narrower definitions of "impartial arbitrator and mediator." However, being an arbitrator between clients is not a function that a lawyer likes to perform. An arbitrator has to be impartial, not only detached in judgment but willing to decide the case adversely to the party who is wrong according to law. An arbritrator's verdict necessarily condemns the loser as it vindicates the winner. For both financial and moral reasons, a lawyer does not want to get into the position of having to condemn someone who has been a client.

"Mediation" does not necessarily involve so polarized a relationship. It can entail adjustment and de-escalation of defined positions, which is what the Code apparently contemplates. But it may mean various kinds of more fluid and positive intercession before the point has been reached where positions are defined. If the latter connotation is accepted, the role is essentially that of "lawyer for the situation."

"Situations" can arise in different ways. Two or more people who have not been clients may bring a "situation" to a lawyer. Sometimes a client who has a lawyer will become involved in a transaction with a third party who does not, and the transaction is one that ought to be handled as a "situation." Most commonly, perhaps, a lawyer may find himself in a "situation" involving clients that he has previously served in separate transactions or relationships. In this circumstance the lawyer, if he properly can, will intercede before the transaction between his clients reaches counterposed positions. Doing so is in his interest, because that way he can retain both clients.

Having a lawyer act for the situation is also in the clients' interests, if adjustment on fair terms is possible, because head-on controversy is expensive and aggravating. A lawyer who failed to avoid a head-on controversy, given reasonable opportunity to do so, will have failed in what his clients generally regard as one of his chief functions—"preventive" legal assistance.

If Brandeis was wrong, then "lawyering for the situation" is marginally illicit professional conduct because it violates the principle of unqualified loyalty to client. But if Brandeis was right, and the record of good practitioners testifies to that conclusion, then what is required is not interdiction of "lawyering for the situation" but reexamination of what is meant by loyalty to client. That is, loyalty to client, like loyalty to country, may take different forms.

It is not easy to say exactly what a "lawyer for the situation" does. Clearly, his functions vary with specific circumstances. But there are common threads. The beginning point is that no other lawyer is immediately involved. Hence, the lawyer is no one's partisan and, at least up to a point, everyone's confidant. He can be the only person who knows the whole situation. He is an analyst of the relationship between the clients, in that he undertakes to discern the needs, fears, and expectations of each and to discover the concordances among them. He is an interpreter, translating inarticulate or exaggerated claims and forewarnings into temperate and mutually intelligible terms of communication. He can contribute historical perspective, objectivity, and foresight into the parties' assessment of the situation. He can discourage escalation of conflict and recruitment of outside allies. He can articulate general principles and common

LAWYER FOR THE SITUATION

custom as standards by which the parties can examine their respective claims. He is advocate, mediator, entrepreneur, and judge, all in one. He could be said to be playing God.

Playing God is a tricky business. It requires skill, nerve, detachment, compassion, ingenuity, and the capacity to sustain confidence. When mishandled, it generates the bitterness and recrimination that results when a deep trust has been betrayed. Perhaps above all, it requires good judgment as to when such intercession can be carried off without unfairly subordinating the interests of one of the parties or having later to abort the mission.

When a relationship between the clients is amenable to "situation" treatment, giving it that treatment is perhaps the best service a lawyer can render to anyone. It approximates the ideal forms of intercession suggested by the models of wise parent or village elder. It provides adjustment of difference upon a wholistic view of the situation rather than bilaterally opposing ones. It rests on implicit principles of decision that express commonly shared ideals in behavior rather than strict legal right. The basis of decision is mutual assent and not external compulsion. The orientation in time tends to be a hopeful view of the future rather than an angry view of the past. It avoids the loss of personal autonomy that results when each side commits his cause to his own advocate. It is the opposite of "going to law."

One would think that the role of "lawyer for the situation" would have been idealized by the bar in parity with the roles of partisan advocate and confidential advisor. The fact that it has not been may itself be worth exploring.

It is clear that a "lawyer for the situation" has to identify clearly his role as such, a requirement that Brandeis conceded he might not always have fulfilled. But beyond saying that he will undertake to represent the best interests of all, a lawyer cannot say specifically what he will do or what each of the clients should do in the situation. (If the outcome of the situation were clearly foreseeable, presumably the lawyer's intercession would be unnecessary.) Moreover, he cannot define his role in the terms of the direction of his effort, for his effort will not be vectored outward toward third persons but will aim at an interaction among the clients. Hence, unlike advocacy or legal counselling involving a single client, lawyering for a situation is not provided with a structure of goals and constraints imposed from outside. The lawyer and the clients must create that structure for themselves, with the lawyer being an active participant. And like the other participants he cannot reveal all that is on his mind or all that he suspects the others may have on their minds, except as doing so aids movement of the situation along lines that seem productive.

A lawyer can proceed in this role only if the clients trust him and, equally important, he trusts himself. Trust is by definition ineffable. It is an acceptance of another's act without demanding that its bona fides be objectively provable; to demand its proof is to confess it does not exist. It is a relationship that is uncomfortable for the client but perhaps even more so for the lawyer. Experienced as he is with the meanness that people can display to each other, why should the lawyer not doubt his own susceptibility to the same failing? But trust is involved also in the role of confidential advisor and advocate. Why should lawyers regard their own trustworthiness as more vulnerable in those roles that in the role of "lawyer for the situation"?

Perhaps it is because the legal profession has succeeded in defining the roles of confidential advisor and advocate in ways that substantially reduce the burden of being trustworthy in these roles. The confidential advisor is told that he may not act to disclose anything about the client, except an announced intention to commit a crime. Short of this extremity, the rules of role have it that the counsellor has no choices to make between the interests of his client and the interests of others. His commitment is to the client alone.

LAWYER FOR THE SITUATION

Correlatively, the advocate is told that he may assert any claim on behalf of a client except one based on fabricated evidence or one empty of any substance at all. Short of this extremity, the advocate also has no choices to make.

The "lawyer for the situation," on the other hand, has choices to make that obviously can go against the interest of one client or another, as the latter perceives it. A lawyer who assumes to act as intercessor has to evoke complete confidence that he will act justly in the circumstances. This is to perform the role of the administered justice itself, but without the constraints inherent in that process (such as the fact that the rules are written down, that they are administered by independent judges, and that outcomes have to be justified by references to reason and precedent). The role of lawyer for the situation therefore may be too prone to abuse to be explicitly sanctioned. A person may be entrusted with it only if he knows that in the event of miscarriage he will have no protection from the law. In this respect, acting as lawyer for the situation can be thought of as similar to a doctor's "authority" to terminate the life of a hopeless patient: It can properly be undertaken only if it will not be questioned afterwards. To this extent Brandeis's critics may have been right.

Yet it seems possible to define the role of intercessor, just as it has been possible to define the role of the trustee or guardian. The role could be defined by contrast with those of confidential counsellor and advocate, perhaps to the advantage of clarity in defining all three.[2] At minimum, a

---

2. The "securities bar" (lawyers handling stock issues sold publicly) has been deeply embroiled in the question of the nature and extent of the obligation of the lawyer for a securities issuer concerning the veracity of statements made by the issuer. One analysis of the problem is that there is conflict over whether the lawyer should be regarded as representing the issuer or as representing the situation of an issuance of stock. See Sommer, "The Emerging Responsibilities of the Securities Lawyer," 1974–75 *Fed. Sec. L. Rep.* par. 79,631.

recognition of the role of lawyer for the situation could result in a clearer perception by both clients and lawyers of one very important and socially estimable function that lawyers can perform and do perform.[3]

3. See Paul, "A New Role for Lawyers in Contract Negotiations," 62 *A.B.A.J.* 93 (1976).

5. Conflict of Interest

"Who is the client?" and "lawyer for the situation" are variations of a more general problem, that of conflict of interest. The question of client identity arises when a group—a corporation, a partnership, a family—that has been collectively treated as a single client has an encounter resulting in legal tensions within the group. When the bonds of common interest suffer such strain that the group can no longer be treated as a unit, the client has to be disaggregated and its members treated as separate clients. On the other hand, the question of "lawyering for the situation" arises when individuals who have divergent interests may nevertheless be better served if the lawyer orchestrates a course of action designed to benefit them all. If the strains of divergent interest make it impossible to continue such a course of action, the "situation" collapses and along with it the role that the lawyer has assumed.

A similar problem arises when a lawyer is asked to serve two clients whose interests already diverge. This is an everyday problem for independent law firms. Most large law firms serve many different clients. Many try to maintain a "portfolio" of clients in which no single client accounts for more than 5 percent of the firm's business. If a client accounts for more than this, the firm's reputation for independence may be cast in doubt. Furthermore, the possibility that the dominant client may withdraw and go elsewhere threatens the firm's solvency. A firm that has many clients, however, faces correspondingly intricate conflict of interest problems, particularly when the clientele includes large corporations with far-flung and constantly changing business involvements. It is often a nice question of judgment whether there is a conflict among the interests of clients. At the same time, avoidance of embarrassing conflicts is critically important in maintaining a firm's reputation for integrity.

Conflicts of interest fall into three general categories: Litigation; bargaining; and what may be called positional conflicts. The first two are directly recognized in the rules of the legal profession, although in a way that does not adequately comprehend their nature. They are talked of here. The problem of positional conflicts is considered in the next chapter.

Litigation

Litigation conflicts are often clearly identifiable. A lawyer who represents a plaintiff cannot also represent a defendant, nor may a lawyer representing one client take on another who plans a lawsuit against the first. A lawyer or firm representing one claimant to a limited fund being administered by a court, such as a decendent's estate or assets in bankruptcy, cannot represent another person whose claim is directly competitive. Beyond these simply stated situations, however, are many that are more problematic.

Plaintiffs with apparently compatible interests may actually be competitive with each other. For example, suppose a disaster occurs in which many people are injured. If all succeed in obtaining large awards, the total claims may exceed the defendant's available insurance and other assets, in which event the claims would be clearly competitive. The same competition can exist even in small disasters such as automobile accidents, if, as often happens, the defendant's only asset is insurance with a relatively low limit of liability. More subtle competition can exist even when the defendants' assets are sufficient, because the claims of several plaintiffs

CONFLICT OF INTEREST

can reduce each other's shock and sympathy value: If one child in a school bus is disfigured, the claim may be a realizable value of $100,000, but if ten are disfigured the realizable value may be less than $1 million. Should one lawyer agree to take all ten cases? His resolution of that question is complicated by the fact that in the economics of litigation the lawyer can get a better return on his time if he takes all ten. For this reason, there is also involved a conflict between the lawyer on the one hand and his clients on the other. The same competition can arise with respect to any group of plaintiffs, such as stockholders, civil rights claimants, and creditors.

Similar problems are presented in litigation involving multiple defendants. When two or more defendants are sued, it is in their interest to maintain a common front if they can, for otherwise each may wind up helping the plaintiff throw blame where he can. But it is in the interest of each defendant to divert to the other such blame as may be found. May one lawyer represent both defendants? The same problem can arise in criminal cases. This was illustrated during the Watergate prosecution when it was concluded—tardily it would seem—that Mr. Ehrlichman and Mr. Haldeman should not be represented by the same lawyer.

The situation is still more ambiguous when litigation is in contemplation but has not yet been commenced. If the plaintiffs have alternative ways of formulating their claims and selecting their targets, there can be a conflict of interest in whether to assert their claims one way rather than another. A recent corporate law suit involved such a situation: Redress could be sought on behalf of several plaintiffs either by way of damages, which would produce an immediate payment, or through a reorganization of the defendant company, which would produce a larger, but delayed, payment. Some plaintiffs wanted money quickly (so did plaintiff's lawyer, for that was where his fee was to come from), others wanted the reorganization. Similar problems are encountered every day in controversies involving multiple creditors. When can one lawyer represent them all?

From the viewpoint of multiple defendants, impending litigation is even more uncertain. Until the litigation begins they do not know who will be sued or on what grounds. The positions that might be taken on their behalf in negotiations over the claim, for example, are necessarily uncertain and the subject of potential conflict.

The dynamics of multiparty litigation, therefore, involve incentives for harmonizing the interests of parties not directly opposed to each other but also corresponding possibilities for suppressing important differences between them. Whether there is harmony or dissonance cannot be determined simply from the objective facts, even if they could be fully known. The clients' attitudes are also relevant and so is the lawyer's approach to the case. The problem is further complicated by the possibility of change in the client's circumstances while the litigation is being pursued. Lawsuits involving large corporations often go on for years; legal relationships between them and other corporations and government regulatory agencies endure for decades. The client's orientation to pending or potential litigation can change as a result of shift in relationships not directly related to the litigation, so that harmony of interest can be transformed into conflict and vice versa. These possibilities can often be only dimly foreseen. How far should a firm go in avoiding the risk of conflict that might eventually occur, when the consequence of being absolutely safe is the refusal of professional business that a client wants to tender and the firms wants to accept?

Still another complication can arise from change in the firm itself. If a member or associate of the firm leaves to join the firm that is representing an opposing litigant, does it follow that one or both firms become disqualified? What if the litigation involves a corporation and a government agency? This problem is further considered in chapter 8.

Bargaining

Conflict of interest problems in litigation have endless variations of which the foregoing are only illustrations. Conflicts of interest in bargaining situations arise in even greater variety. The prototype situation is that of private bilateral negotiation of a contract for future performance, where the parties are set against each other in seeking advantageous terms. Negotiation to settle a past dispute involves similar conflicts of interest. Negotiation with a government agency over the terms of proposed government action is still another, and so is negotiation in and around the legislative process. Bargaining can be bilateral or multilateral and when multilateral can involve groups whose members' interests coincide to a greater or lesser degree. It can involve third parties who are more or less neutrals. The process can involve relatively open disclosure and a quest for objectively "reasonable" terms, or it can closely resemble poker. A bargain can be pursued in an isolated transaction between parties who have had no past relationships with each other and expect none in the future (a merger of two corporations is often of this character), or as a phase of a continuing relationship (as is usual in labor negotiations, for example). Given all these variables, when should it be said that two clients have interests that diverge to the point of "conflict"?

In all these situations, when there is an irrepressible conflict of interest it is a violation of professional duty for a lawyer to try to act for "the situation." If there is no real conflict, the lawyer who insists that each party be separately represented imposes needless expense and distress on the parties. Such an insistence is little different from stirring up litigation or overcharging the clients, both of which are unethical.

We have seen that in some bargaining relationships, a lawyer can act as a mediator-arbitrator-orchestrator for all the parties, as "lawyer for the situation." On the other hand, some bargaining relationships involve irrepressible conflict of interest between the parties involved—for example, negotiation aimed at settling a claim of fraud. The propriety of a lawyer's conduct in representing "the situation" turns on distinguishing one kind of bargaining relationship from the other, but the distinction is often not very clear.

One factor in making the distinction is cost. If the transaction involves a lot of money, each party usually can justify the expense of retaining its own legal adviser and the only question is whether that should be done. If the transaction involves limited stakes, however, separate representation can increase the legal overhead to a burdensom or prohibitive level. It seems evident that this ought to be a relevant consideration, but how it should be taken into account so far as the lawyer is concerned is not so easy to say. How much overhead is too much obviously does not admit of clear definition.

As the rules stand, however, a lawyer is not regarded as having a duty to define his role as "lawyer for the situation," rather than partisan, in order to spare legal costs for someone who cannot afford them. The emphasis given to avoidance of conflict of interest actually obscures such an approach to the problem. Yet it seems perfectly tenable that a lawyer should have a positive duty to act "for the situation" whenever he can, in order to reduce costs. The cost problem is not often presented in transactions between large corporations, or between a corporation and the government, because they always have their lawyers review their contracts. But in that context the question can be whether participation by an independent law firm is indicated and, if so, what role the independent firm ought to play.

Another factor is whether the transaction in question is one that admits of open-ended possibilities. Some bargains may be expected to conform to terms established by custom or business usage. Certain types of real estate transactions and lending agreements fall in this category, for example. Other bargains as a practical matter have a limited set of possibilities because the constraints upon both parties dictate a narrow range of options. If a debtor has few assets and simple but large debts, for example, there are not many different ways in which his creditors can come to terms with him. On the other hand, when the parties confront an open-ended bargaining possibility, the definition of a "fair" bargain can reduce itself to the resultant of an arm's length bargaining process. The bargaining process is then a struggle for marginal advantage in which a critical element is bluff—a pretense of intractability masking an undisclosed degree of willingness to make concessions. When a lawyer is called on to bargain for a party, he shares the party's mask and the party's secret real intentions. He obviously cannot do that simultaneously for both parties.

A third and vital factor is the bargaining "style" that the parties seem predisposed to adopt. Some parties, at least in some circumstances, prefer a bargaining process that purports to aim at an objectively "fair and reasonable" outcome. In other circumstances, by preference or in default of an alternative, the parties engage in a contentious struggle characterized by posturing, psychological harrassment, and dissimulation, not unlike embittered litigation. Parties adopting the former style can usually be assumed to be more ready to accommodate or repress conflict than those who come in growling.

Still another factor, which arises in bargaining as in litigation, is the possibility that circumstances may change during the course of carrying out the bargain. A simple example: A firm represents a borrower in a loan secured by a corporate mortgage; can that firm later represent a lender in a subsequent loan to that borrower, especially if the second loan requires renegotiation of the original mortgage?

If the variations of cost, bargaining latitude, bargaining style, and possibility of changed circumstances are taken into account, the range of possible conflicts in bargaining situations is very great. At one end of the continuum is the small transaction with stereotyped terms negotiated openly between parties whose future relationship is predictable. At the other end is the large complicated transaction, unique in type, combatively negotiated in unstable circumstances. In the former, there is no conflict of interest between the clients; in the latter there clearly is. In cases falling between these extremes, there is only doubt.

According to the official rules, the lawyer may resolve this doubt in favor of representing both parties if the conflict will not affect his "professional judgment" on behalf of each client and if he makes "full disclosure" to the clients and obtains their consent to the dual representation. There are serious difficulties with this approach. One of them, the "full disclosure" requirement, has already been considered. The point was that "full" disclosure is impossible if the lawyer elicits full communication from each client and fully observes his duty of confidentiality to both. What must be meant by "full disclosure," therefore, is "adequate disclosure." This means that the disclosure may be limited and that the lawyer has to decide how far it should go.

The second difficulty is that focussing on the effect of the conflict on the lawyer's "professional judgment" seems to deflect attention from the real issues.

First, it has to be asked what is meant by "professional judgment." Although the rules do not define the concept, it may be taken to mean the following: A lawyer's professional

CONFLICT OF INTEREST

judgment is his analysis of the legal and practical dimensions of a client's position, evaluation of the risks and potential gains involved in pursuing alternative courses of action to improve the position, and recommendations of what the lawyer believes to be the optimal course of action for the client to take. Given this definition, according to the Code of Professional Responsibility, the question then is: Is the situation such that the lawyer can make a legal analysis, evaluation, and recommendation for each client in terms that are not incompatible with the analysis, evaluation, and recommendation made for the other?

This puts the cart before the horse. It is only after the lawyer has made such an analysis that he can determine whether the optimal courses for each client would, if pursued, collide. Furthermore, the question is whether, in leading up to the point of possible collision, the lawyer would have to *act* for one client in a fashion antagonistic to the interests of the other—that is, as advocate rather than as arbitrator or intercessor.

Thus, if the lawyer concluded that two of his clients should sue each other, he could not appear as courtroom advocate for both. The conclusion, however, does not result from the fact that his professional judgment was impaired in deciding that litigation was probable or inevitable; it follows from the facts that in litigation the lawyering role for each client is that of advocate and that in the adversary system the lawyer cannot serve as advocate for both sides.

Alternatively, the lawyer might conclude that the interests of two of his clients irreconcilably conflict but should be arbitrated. The lawyer could not serve as each client's advocate in arbitration, any more than he could do so in a courtroom. However, he could properly assume the role of arbitrator. He might decide against assuming such a role, but this would not be because the role would affect his "professional judgment." His disinclination to serve as arbitrator between clients results from the effect on his clients of his acting as such. If he properly performed the role of arbitrator and thus were perfectly neutral between the clients, he might alienate the client against whom he made his award, and would alienate that client even more if it was suspected that the lawyer's judgment as arbitrator was influenced by his desire to keep the other client. However, if the lawyer's analysis indicated that each client should pursue a course compatible with the other client's best course of action, there would be no conflict and he could act as "lawyer for the situation."

The conflict of interest dilemma thus has at least two dimensions. The first is that in any relationship between persons with whom he is interacting in a professional capacity, the lawyer may act as intercessor, mediator, arbitrator, or partisan advocate. Whether there is conflict of interest between the clients depends on which role the lawyer assumes. The second aspect of the problem is: Which role should he assume? In some situations, his role is dictated by external circumstances. If he previously represented a client who then brings suit through other counsel against another of his clients, the lawyer can only represent the latter. (Indeed, he may not be able to do even that if the litigation concerns a matter upon which he had given advice to the former client.) But if the relationship between the clients is more ambiguous, the lawyer's range of possibly appropriate roles is correspondingly broader. And an important element of ambiguity is how the clients contemplate going about dealing with the potential conflict between them.

Clients do not have a conflict of interest simply because their interests diverge or because an intense legal dispute could arise between them. If this were true, there would be a conflict of interest between practically everyone whose paths in life might cross. People have conflicts of interest only if, in addition to having divergent interests, one or both wish to pursue them beyond a certain degree of aggression. Whether they wish to do so inevitably depends on circumstances. It also depends on the legal advice they may get, which turns the question into a circle.

In broader terms, the measure of aggression appropriate to the assertion of an interest is also influenced by the social environment, by the particular community's norms of assertiveness, and by the costs incurred in being aggressive. It is thus necessary to look at the problem of conflict of interest in a much larger framework, one that extends to the culture of society. The larger social framework may not perceptibly determine whether interests conflict in a specific situation faced by a lawyer and his clients. But it does influence the social subsystems that the lawyer and his clients find themselves in, subsystems such as the world of corporate finance, of merchant trading, and of relations between regulated industries and regulatory agencies. In these subsystems, the attitude toward conflict very much determines whether divergent interests are viewed as conflicts of interest. Thus, members of a family do not sue each other over use of the family car or, ordinarily at least, over distribution of inheritance. Participants in continuing and close-knit business relationships turn to litigation, turn indeed even to legal advice, only in disputes of more than ordinary complexity, magnitude, or bitterness.

In respect to these broader terms in which conflict of interest is defined, the culture of the law itself is a contributing determinant. The point can be made more clearly by considering cultures that sharply contrast in this regard. In this country, the ideals of due process, private property, and formal equality (that is, equality in legal status) lead to the definition of human relationships in legal terms. They also imply that adjudication is a normal and in some sense an ideal form of resolving disputed relationships. A derivative of this premise is that the role of partisan advocate and counsellor is a normal, primary, and perhaps idealized one for a lawyer to play. By way of sharp contrast, in Japanese culture the ideals of concord and deference to traditional authority predominate. The definition of human relationships in legal terms is regarded as the exhibition of something like antisocial tendencies. A derivative of this premise is that in Japan it is uncommon to resort to legal assistance and more uncommon still for lawyers to assume the role of partisan rather than of neutral expositor of the law. Within both countries, certainly this one, the degree of "legalism" in definition of relationships varies with specific context, as already suggested. But when an American lawyer is consulted, the client's orientation to the problem is usually adversarial, precisely because the lawyer's normal or expected role is that of partisan. Hence, the fact that a client has consulted a lawyer can signify that the client contemplates a legally assertive course of action and itself is a step in the direction of defining a divergency of interest as a conflict if interest.

This means that when a lawyer is consulted by a client, he ordinarily must assume that if the client's interest diverges from the interest of another, a conflict of interest exists between them. Nevertheless, the lawyer must also consider the possibility that there is no conflict. It is in his interest to do so, because on the assumption he can serve both clients. It is in the clients' interest that he do so, for having a "lawyer for the situation" is usually cheaper, quicker, and less acrimonious than defining the problem in such a way that each party has to have separate counsel. Moreover, when the client is a large corporation or goverment agency, consultation with a lawyer does not necessarily signal the existence of a conflict in the same way as consultation by an "ordinary" client. This is because these organizations customarily subject all important transactions to legal review as a matter of course.

CONFLICT OF INTEREST

A different kind of dilemma faces the lawyer even before he reaches the point of deciding what his role in a situation should be. It arises from the fact that in order to assess the situation, and thereby determine what role he might have to play, he has to find out what the situation is. His dilemma arises from three converging rules that govern his information gathering. First, nothing he learns from a client may be used adversely to the client's interest. Second, everything he knows and learns about the situation is a resource in performing service for a client; any lesser use of available knowledge would be lack of zeal. Third, it is fraud to induce confidential disclosures, such as a client makes to an attorney, unless it is clear that they will be kept confidential. But whether information is to be helpful or harmful to a client and whether it may be communicated to others depends on the role that the lawyer is to play in using it. Hence, when the lawyer is trying to find out what the situation is so that he can define his professional role, he has to make assumptions both as to what the situation is and as to what role he might play. In doing so, of course, he runs the risk that the assumptions he has made at any point may later turn out to be untenable.

In judging whether a conflict exists, the large law firm faces special difficulties. One is simply that of identifying possible conflicts. A large law firm's inventory of pending matters runs literally into the hundreds and perhaps thousands of separate transactions. Both the inventory as a whole and the character of each item is in constant change. The internal organization of most large law firms is highly decentralized, the work being done by individual lawyers or small groups clustered in more or less loosely organized departments. In some firms, some of the partners have intimate, long-term relationships with particular clients, acting in isolation from their partners and thus making communication about pending matters very difficult. The risk of conflict rises exponentially with the size of the firm, the degree of decentralization, and the extent of insularity within the firm. To meet the risk, all large firms have "new matters" procedures: weekly review of the inventory by a committee, intraoffice bulletins, informal cross-checking, and "smell."

The large firm also faces a difficult problem in formulating judgments about conflicts. Members of a firm have different standards of punctillio, different degrees of aversion to the risk of conflict, different concerns for maintaining or expanding the firm's clientele and fee revenue. Sensitivity to conflict therefore varies among them. The question often is: "Do you trust your partner?" One way to minimize the strains on trust and to coordinate the firm's policy is to have, as one participant's firm does, a "two partner" rule: A close or troublesome question as to whether there is a conflict must be decided jointly by the partner directly in charge and by at least one other partner. Another procedure, more bureaucratic, is to refer all questions of conflict to the firm's management committee. Still another, more hierarchical, is to refer them to "the" senior partner. But of course the problem remains, what is a close or troublesome case?

Another problem is the severity of the consequences to a large firm when its involvement in a matter has become far advanced before a conflict is detected. The clients or large corporate firms are relatively sophisticated about conflicts and reasonably tolerant of wholly unforeseeable ones. But they are also in a position to wreak heavy retribution if their affairs become involved in a conflict they think should have been avoided. Withdrawal of their business can severely disturb the firm's fortunes, which is a gentle way of saying it can result in loss of employment. Word of the client's dissatisfaction can spread through the corporate grapevine, resulting in permanent damage to the firm's reputation and the reputations of each of its members and associates. And even an expression of annoyance can disturb a lawyer-client relationship.

CONFLICT OF INTEREST

Involvement in a really serious conflict of interest is feared by a large law firm more than anything except encountering personal dishonesty in its membership. The risk of conflict attends a firm's practice at every turn. Identifying a potential conflict and deciding whether and how the firm may proceed requires constant vigilance and careful discretion.

In one sense, however, conflict of interest between clients is a self-proving event. If the client thinks there is a conflict, there is a conflict. A client will assume there is no conflict, unless he discovers it or if the firm has called the possibility to his attention. When the client himself discovers a conflict, it represents a mistake by the firm, for the firm should have seen it before the client did. Good firms do not like making mistakes. Hence, the lawyers in the firm have to anticipate not only what they regard as conflicts but also what their clients will think are conflicts. It is for the lawyer to raise the question if it is to be raised at all. When to do so generally requires a most delicate professional judgment, for to raise the question is to make some kind of disclosure about another client's affairs, begetting another set of difficulties.

Deciding whether a conflict exists may well be instinctual in the same way that deciding upon the identity of the client is a matter of "instinct"—that is, the decision is quick, multifactored, necessarily ill-informed, and sometimes involves dangerously high stakes. But it seems possible to state in rational terms what the decision involves.

First, the question is not whether the situation "is" one of conflict of interest. The question is whether the lawyer should approach the situation that way and define his relationship to the clients accordingly.

Second, the question is whether the situation properly should be treated as a "one lawyer" matter, in which the lawyer acts as intercessor, or a "two lawyer" matter, in which each party will have a lawyer acting as partisan counsellor and advocate. The question of which role to assume itself requires "professional judgment," and indeed requires a kind of professional judgment that encompasses all other kinds of professional judgment. This is because the lawyer, in deciding which role to assume, has to think through what he could do for each client in each of the alternative roles that he might assume.

Third, the "answer" to the question itself involves another conflict. From the client's point of view, other things being equal, it is more advantageous to have his lawyer act as intercessor instead of as partisan, because the latter involves the more costly "two lawyer" procedure. From the lawyer's point of view, being an intercessor is more risky, because it involves the heavy responsibility of being and seeming fair to everyone.

One word more on conflict of interest. It was noted earlier that a lawyer can do things for his clients that are prohibited by the rules of professional ethics, such as lying, helping carry out a fraud, or destroying evidence. These measures, if they can be gotten away with, can be very helpful to a client. Some clients in some circumstances plainly expect their lawyers to perform such services; this is evidently what John Mitchell had in mind in directing that the surveillance operations which culminated in Watergate be under a lawyer's direction.[1] But if a client wants dirty tricks performed, a conflict of interest arises if his lawyer is not disposed to perform them.

The reaction at Seven Springs to such a suggestion was sharp and immediate, apparently all the way around: You simply do not do such things. There is no reason to doubt the sincerity of this affirmation or the fact that the participants guided their own conduct accordingly. But there is some reason to wonder about the mechanisms for handling

1. Or so John Dean has indicated. Dean, *Blind Ambition* 74-76 (1976).

the problem of "dirty tricks," for surely that problem pervades real life.

If dirty tricks with the law are involved, the problem of dealing with them is often handled by shifting the assignment away from the organization's regular lawyers. Several observers of the profession have noted, for example, that large corporations sometimes retain small, local law firms to handle real property taxes and zoning problems, and also the fact that these matters often involve more or less open bribery of officials. Again, the illegal political payments in Watergate were usually handled by "special counsel," a euphemism for bagman. One suspects also that by common but tacit consent, a lot of shady legal matters are kept away from the law firm and legal department and handled by operatives whose own form of self-righteousness is that they are not hypocrites.

Still another way to cope with the problem is to redefine it so that a satisfactory resolution is possible without overt violation of the canons of ethics. For example, it is unethical to counsel the systematic destruction of records that might eventually be embarrassing under the antitrust or tax laws; it is not unethical to provide a projection of the legal aspects of a records retention policy. Telling an employee that he should forget certain conservations is unethical; advising him of the legal consequences that might follow from certain kinds of conversation is not. And so on. The cynical ideal would be to formulate a problem in a way that is perfectly ethical from the lawyer's viewpoint and perfectly opportunistic from the client's viewpoint. And because corporate clients and corporate lawyers are both sophisticated, that ideal can be much more easily realized than in situations in which a naive client cannot grasp what the lawyer is trying to avoid.

No doubt there is a lot of this in the grist of corporate law practice. Yet the incidence may be less than would be inferred from folklore. While there are gains in being a near-shyster, there are also costs—loss of self-esteem, loss of credibility, loss of reputation for competence in delicate matters, and perhaps even legal liability. And there are counterpart risks for the clients. Generally speaking, lawyers for large corporations proceed on the assumption that everything they do is done in a goldfish bowl. Yet it can remain possible that every client hopes, if a moment of extremity should be reached, that his lawyer will fix the judge, while every lawyer wants it believed that he would not. So also, it is possible that every client fears, if a moment of extremity should be reached, that his lawyer will abandon him. That fear is not groundless for, as Thurman Arnold is said to have said, "If it comes down to whether you go to jail or your client does, make sure it's the client." That, too, is a conflict of interest.

6. Unpopular Clients

The theory of practice in the law is that any client can obtain the services of any lawyer unless that lawyer is barred from serving him because of a conflict of interest. The theory has two corollaries. One is that the client's inability to pay is not a proper reason for a lawyer to refuse him help. The other is that the unpopularity of the client's cause is not a proper basis for such a refusal. The legal profession attaches much importance to these principles partly because the profession itself thinks its monopoly of the practice of law depends on them.

The legal profession is surely worthier for holding the aspiration to serve the poor and the despised, even if it falls well short of fulfilling that aspiration. It is not clear, however, why professing and seeking to fulfill the ideal has any connection to the profession's monopoly of the practice of law in this day and age. There would be such a connection if lawyers made up a small band of gentlemen practitioners whose aid was indispensable to obtaining justice. If that were so, a person who could not get one of the company of lawyers to take his case would have no case. Further, the company of lawyers could make monopolists' profits in serving the affluent, from which to pay the cost of rendering service to the poor.

Such a monopoly existed in many communities at one time, and still exists in some smaller communities. But liberal admission to the legal profession has much weakened the monopoly. Although no one except a licensed lawyer may render legal services, there are so many lawyers of such varied political persuasions that "the company" has no policy of exclusion toward legal but unpopular causes. So far as the poor are concerned, it is now simply romanticism to think that legal services can be provided to the poor out of a surplus that lawyers earn from the rich. There are too many poor, with needs that are too great, to be served through the vagaries of charity.

The legal profession's ideal of public service still holds sway, however. A cynical view is not required to see that the profession's avowal of the ideal has practical uses. It carries with it a claim of special place in determining the operation of such services as legal aid and the Federal Legal Services Program, which are perceived by the bar as providing help to the poor as surrogates for the legal profession. (In this respect, the claims of the legal profession regarding legal services parallel the claims of doctors regarding medical services.) The ideal of public service helps sustain the claim of special place in regulating the profession—matters of legal education, bar examinations, disciplinary proceedings, etc. More fundamentally, it sustains the idea that the lawyer in serving a client is a neutral and a mere agent, and therefore not responsible for the direction or consequences of the causes in whose service he is enlisted. The extent to which that idea is sustainable is of no little importance to the self-concept of the modern corporation lawyer.

So far as concerns legal assistance to the poor, charitable services by practicing lawyers, is now mostly a matter of tokenism. In this respect, charity in legal services has followed the way of charity in medicine, charity in schooling, and charity in food and clothing—a small and needed supplement to a major undertaking in publicly financed welfare. The problem remains for lawyers, and for citizens, what size token they will give. Some have talked of a tithing. Many actually give only a pittance, either in time or in money. The size of the token is of consequence, however, for it says what

UNPOPULAR CLIENTS

a person will do for others when he does not have to do anything.

The problem of unpopular causes is more complicated. The theory that a lawyer has an obligation to a cause even if it is unpopular no doubt originates with the fact that acting as lawyer for such a cause can be very unpleasant. The theory is sustained by the fact that it submerges the lawyer's responsibility for a cause into the purposes of his client. The character of the lawyer's service on behalf of a client, said still to be practiced by English barristers, is epitomized in the metaphor of a cab driver: He takes whomever beckons to whatever destination may be commanded. The lawyer is, to be sure, subject to restrictions on his course of action, in that there are forms of assistance he is prohibited from rendering, for example, subornation of perjury, harrassing litigation, etc. Within these limits, the lawyer is considered merely an agent, whether in litigation or in bargaining. The medium of his agency is his technical art, and his technical art is "the law."

The description is at variance with real life. It assumes that the law is a settled and acknowledged body of rules. It assumes that the lawyer as advocate in court simply helps the judge "understand" the rules and "discover" their application to specific situations. It assumes that the lawyer as counsellor takes the rules as fixed channels into which transactions must be fitted. It ignores altogether the role of the lawyer as lobbyist. Most important, it ignores the fact that legal rules are now recognized as being more or less uncertainly positioned guidelines in a large field of forces. These forces include general normative concepts of equality, utility, property, and charity, and the realities of political and economic power. The location of a legal rule's boundaries at any given time is the resultant of these vectors.

If this is a correct analysis of "the law," it means that

lawyers necessarily are to some degree political actors. They are the spokesmen, in litigation and in bargaining, for the various social and economic factions that invoke normative claims and exercise power to keep the boundaries of the law where they are, or to relocate them. A position adopted by a lawyer on behalf of a client thus influences, even if in a small way, the configuration of the law itself. A position adopted by a lawyer on behalf of one client is therefore significant for other clients. A lawyer who asserts a position for one client can assert an opposite position for another only at the cost of neutralizing his effectiveness for both.

The result is that a lawyer can have positional conflicts of interest. He can find himself being asked to assert legal positions on behalf of a client which if successfully established or maintained will adversely transform the legal framework within which another client conducts his affairs. The likelihood of this interaction increases if the lawyer is in a firm, if the firm has a large number of clients, and if the clients are involved in legal controversies that have important political or economic implications. This, rather than something simpler and perhaps more sinister, explains why positional conflicts of interest are a real possibility, particularly if the clients are involved in legal controversies that have important socioeconomic implications.

For a large law firm, positional conflicts are inevitable. Some positional conflicts are normal and accepted by firms and clients alike, as one of the consequences of employing an independent law firm. Thus, in tax litigation a firm would not be regarded as having an improper positional conflict if it took the position for one client that certain revenue was ordinary income and for another client that similar revenue was capital gain. It would not be improper to take the position for one client that certain assets of a company were subject to a mortgage and take the position for another client that similar assets of another company were not subject to an identical mortgage—unless the firm itself drafted the mortgage. In these and other situations in which members of the corporate business community as a whole find themselves sometimes on one side of a legal controversy, sometimes on another, positions taken on their behalf are regarded as neutral, as indeed they are in the larger context of political economy. Other positions, however, involve polarity between the interests of business clientele and other types of clients. For a firm whose clients are mostly corporations, a serious question is posed in representing clients whose legal positions are mostly opposed to those of business.

The firm can approach the question with either of two minds. One way that some firms deal with positional conflict is to shape their whole practice so that it is avoided. Thus, in labor law there are "management" firms and "labor" firms. In personal injury litigation, there are plaintiffs' lawyers and defense lawyers, the latter invariably having continuing ties to the liability insurance industry. In corporate litigation there are firms that specialize in plaintiff causes in antitrust and stockholder litigation, and other firms that only defend such matters. Some such orientations of a firm's practice are infused with a heavy ideological element. There are "radical lawyers" who defend political dissidents, "public interest" firms that represent what they consider to be the public interest, and silk stocking firms that serve only what they consider to be the carriage trade.

Lawyers and law firms that adopt this approach to positional conflicts pay a price for doing so. The price is that their reputation for professional independence is comprised, for their judgments on legal questions are assumed to be a product of a fixed position rather than a politically nonpartisan analysis of the matter involved. These firms accept the polarization of their practice and indeed often regard it as a source of attraction for clientele: "A good, sound corporate firm"; "a really dedicated fighter for the individual."

Many firms, however, do not want to accept such a one-sided identity. It conflicts with the profession's traditional ideal. It diminishes their credibility when they try to assert novel or difficult positions based on "the law." It makes them less attractive places of employment for circumspective young lawyers. It blurs the indistinct line between being a lawyer and being a politician. Many firms therefore take on matters involving positions and ideologies that conflict with those of their general clientele. When they do so, they are often more effective than counsel identified with the position to be asserted on behalf of the client. Many of Louis Brandeis's businessmen clients discovered this, as did many clients who were represented by big law firms in the "loyalty-security" controversies of the McCarthy era. There is also a price, however, for asserting positional freedom. Some clients do not like it at all.

The legal profession has officially recognized the problem of positional conflicts only to the extent of saying that a lawyer should not refuse to serve a client because his cause is unpopular. This is an important principle and one not easily given full effect. "Unpopular cause" in this context means one attended by obloquy, such as defense of blacks accused of interracial crimes in the South in years past, suits on behalf of farm laborers in the San Joaquin Valley, defense of Communists, etc. The principle that these causes are entitled to legal assistance has been vindicated by individual lawyers and firms, often at great cost to themselves. The bar itself has been erratic, certainly often timid, in giving support to the principle. For example, special efforts were required to provide fraternal support to lawyers who represented Communists in the 1950s and to civil rights advocates in the South before 1964. Similarly, the bar's attitude toward the Federal Legal Services Program, which assisted causes conflicting with the position of a large part of the bar's regular clientele, was divided and ambivalent at least until 1970. Nevertheless, it seems accurate to say that the principle now enjoys the acquiescence and perhaps even the support of the bar, though there remain many members of the general public who think that only the good guys deserve due process.

Aside from what might be called social causes celebre, the bar recognizes the problem of positional conflict in only one other context. This is in the organization of the profession itself. The bar's organized activities include working for change in the law, which involves drafting and recommending legislation, which in turn involves controversial issues of public policy. Although the bar as a whole is conservative in its political orientation, it has come to accept the existence of political diversity among its members. That in turn has led to more or less open acceptance of the fact that there are plaintiff lawyers and defense lawyers in the personal injury and corporate fields, "management" and "labor" lawyers, civil liberties lawyers and law enforcement lawyers, etc. These identities are acknowledged sub silentio in the organizational structure of the bar, in appointments to bar committees, and in slating candidates for bar association office. Bar politics have thus become a replica of legislative politics, shifted some degrees to the right. While many lawyers still hold with the late Harrison Tweed that client interests should remain at the door of the bar association, most lawyers now take a more realistic if resigned view of the matter.

In the domain of law practice as distinct from bar association affairs, the problem of positional conflicts has two aspects. One has to do with unpopular causes as traditionally defined. The situation is mixed. Some firms, including most of the premier corporate firms these days, take pride in the fact that they will and do handle such cases. Others will handle them when the job to be done is a quiet one, but will not get involved on behalf of such a client—or any client—if the matter is going to be noisy or newsy. Others definitely, but with as little said about it as possible, will not touch them. In any event, in highly visible individual cases, particularly those that attract support of "social cause" interest groups, it is now relatively rare that positional or ideological considerations prevent anyone from getting competent legal assistance. In large urban centers, competent counsel can usually be found to assist in unpopular causes that are not highly visible. When a cause arises in a smaller city or town, however, the local web of social/economic connections can powerfully inhibit a lawyer from being an aggressive champion. For example, in a race discrimination case in a small city in the South, it is still difficult to retain established counsel (meaning a good white lawyer) even in a fee-paying matter. And the problem persists not only in such cases and not only in the South.

The other important class of cases includes causes that are not popularly unpopular but are unpopular with the people at the top of large business corporations. Does a corporate firm want to take a plaintiff's antitrust case? How about an employment discrimination case, given that attorneys fees can be recovered if the case is won? Does it want to defend an income tax evasion case or a criminal fraud prosecution? Professional lore answers these questions affirmatively but professional practice in the elite firms answers them ambivalently. On the one hand, virtually all elite firms affirm the legitimacy of acting as counsel in these cases. On the other hand, they themselves will do so only to a carefully measured extent.

Up to a point, it is advantageous for a corporate law firm to handle remunerative matters involving "antibusiness" positions, just as it is advantageous to do legal aid, public interest work, and politically unpopular cases. As suggested earlier, it improves the firm's reputation for public service, professional conscience, and political independence. It also evidences the integrity of the firm's commitment to a client, a matter of importance to business clients as well as to others. A firm that will defend an outcast political dissident to the hilt can be counted on to defend an outcast corporation to the hilt; a firm that does not flinch from reading the law to an Unamerican Activities Committee will not flinch from reading it to some other investigatory agency. Furthermore, a firm's representation of "antibusiness" positions establishes bonds of some sort with the liberal political establishment, a matter of no little practical importance in Washington and some other seats of government. Beyond a certain point, however, a firm's association with causes that are unpopular in the eyes of the business community raises doubts, in the phrase, as to the firm's soundness. An independent professional is fine, a maverick something else.

The problem for a firm is to maintain balance in its position as a political actor, given whatever is its self-defined political role and its perception of the tipping points of its various clients. An old conservative firm may confine its legal aid work to a dowager's cook. New York and Washington corporate firms will do much more, particularly in civil liberties and civil rights. A firm whose reputation is largely based on its competence in litigation will take cases on any side, as long as the cases are big and tough. A trouble-shooter Washington firm may take all of these and more. A firm in a provincial city may feel it cannot afford any positional conflicts, so powerful are the possibilities of ostracism.

The ideal in modern law practice is no doubt to have a firm that is so good that it can attract and hold a solid paying clientele while also expressing in its practice both social conscience and professional independence. It is not given to many to achieve that measure of competence, and of these not all see the opportunity it presents for professional fulfillment. Perhaps they don't care. Correspondingly, it is not given to many critics of the corporate bar to recognize that a measured fulfillment of the professional ideal is better than none.

7. Fees

The Code of Professional Responsibility treats the subject of fees as a part of the more general question of making legal services available to people. This approach recognizes that the cost of legal services affects their distribution and may imply that restraint in fee-setting is necessary to assure that people can obtain needed legal assistance. On the other hand, the official rules contain no suggestion that lawyers should charge the lowest reasonable fee for a service, or even that they should make their practices efficient so that the cost of service can be reduced.

The rules proscribe "clearly excessive" fees. (One wonders why the proscription does not simply refer to "excessive" fees.) However, the standard for determining a proper fee, and therefore an improper one, involves eight factors. Any eight-factor formula produces a wide range of outcomes, particularly if some of the factors are indeterminate, like those in the Code:

—"time and labor";
—the fee "customarily charged" in that locality;
—the monetary value of the matter for which the service is provided and the result obtained;
—the preemption of other business because of possible conflict of interest;
—the urgency of the matter;
—"nature and length of the professional relationship with the client";
—the experience and reputation of the lawyer;
—whether the fee is fixed or contingent.

Possibly this formula would permit detection of an outrageous fee. However, an outrageous fee could probably be as easily detected without the formula. The courts have not found the formula uniformly serviceable in fixing fees that must have judicial approval, such as those charged to a guardian or a trustee. Courts are sometimes disposed to approve fees in the amount requested, and often do so when the lawyer is court-appointed in a patronage system. In such instances, the Code's formula provides sustaining authority. When a serious review of fees is required, however, the courts usually reduce the problem to two factors: time, in accordance with prevailing hourly rates, and the degree of contingency. It is perhaps noteworthy that this is the basis upon which most lawyers charge their regular clients and upon which the government pays when it retains private counsel.

There are a couple of other matters in the Code that warrant comment. These are practices that if anything put upward pressure on fees. The first is use of the bar association fee schedule. This practice is now outlawed by an antitrust decision of the Supreme Court, but was long observed under the rubric of "customary charges" in the locality.

The other is the referral fee. A nonlawyer cannot be given a fee for referring a case to a lawyer; that is illegal hustling. Neither, theoretically, can a lawyer accept a fee for merely referring a case to another lawyer, for example, when a general practitioner refers a case to a trial specialist. But "division of fees" is permitted, as long as the client is advised that "a division" will be made and the division is proportional to the "services performed and responsibility assumed" by each lawyer. These rules do not require disclosing the terms of the division to the client, nor do they tell how to measure the proportion of "responsibility" between the referring lawyer and the receiving lawyer. In personal injury referrals in many parts of the country, the standard arrangement is that the entire fee is a contingent one-third of the claimant's recovery and that this fee is divided one-third to the referring lawyer and two-thirds to the specialist. The effect of this arrangement is to steer claimants to specialists, which is advantageous for the client, but at a charge that is no doubt higher than the referring lawyer ordinarily gets for his other services.

Legally, the ethical rules proscribing excessive fees are redundant. The law at large fully covers the matter. A contract for a fee is, under general principles of law, a contract between a fiduciary and his protected dependent. As such, it is unenforcable unless its terms are fair to the client. Hence, the rules in the Code go no further than the law of contract and probably stop short of it. So much for the rules.

Fees are the subject of another branch of bar literature as well. This has to do with practices and procedures for charging clients. Broadly speaking, the discussions fall into two headings. One is law office management, a matter we will come to presently. The other can be described only as stock-watering techniques—how to make the client think his case is getting a lot of attention and therefore why it will result in a substantial fee. The techniques include sending the client superfluous reports of case status and progress, calling him outside of business hours to create the impression of overtime work, rendering minutely detailed statements, etc. About the only redeeming thing that can be said for the ethics of these practices is that they are not necessarily incompatible with rendering the client good service at fair value. They can be considered as techniques for overcoming a client's resistance to the fact that some legal services strike laymen as startlingly expensive. This in turn raises the more fundamental question, which has both ethical and economic aspects, of why legal services, or some of them, are expensive.

One explanation is that the bar maintains a conspiracy in restraint of competition, and thus is able to keep the price of its services higher than what could be charged under competitive conditions. With respect to legal services required by low and middle income people, there is more to this suspicion than the bar is willing to concede. The legal profession has succeeding in excluding or reducing competition in many legal services that could be done fairly cheaply. These include writing a will, getting an uncontested divorce, and preparing a real estate deed. Behind the wall of professional monopoly surrounding these services, the members of the bar have maintained forebearance from price competition through such means as fee schedules, prohibition on advertising, and restrictions on how clients may be put in touch with lawyers. These restrictive practices are now under attack from both within profession and outside it, and may well be on their way to demise. But even if they should disappear, all but the most routine kinds of legal services will remain "expensive," that is, they will command relatively high prices.

This became apparent in the Seven Springs discussion of the fees problem. The participants were well positioned to talk to the question intelligently and objectively. Practically all the lawyers present had some kind of experience in setting fees and discussing them with clients. Several of them were responsible for purchasing the services of independent law firms for corporations or government agencies. A few of them had made studies of the comparative costs of retaining independent lawyers and providing legal services through a law department staffed by employee lawyers. Most were acquainted with what has been earlier identified as law office management, a practical science for determining the cost of legal services and making them more efficient.

If the subject brings to mind a counting house rather than chambers, it is nevertheless a necessary and therefore legitimate aspect of the practice of law. Broadly speaking, legal services cost a lot because good legal services are in high demand and limited supply. On the demand side, the strongest generative force by far is the intensive regulating and taxing activity of government. Regulations and taxation impose costs, these days very heavy ones, whose incidence a business aims to minimize, just as it aims to minimize the costs of materials, labor, transportation, and overhead. Lawyers are employed by business to devise operating techniques that constitute compliance with law at lowest cost, and by government to intercept low cost techniques that fall short of legal compliance; other lawyers are employed, as judges, to referee disputes along the law's ever-lengthening borders.

On the supply side, legal services have a high unit cost because they involve personal rather than machine labor, because they are rendered by individuals who want to earn incomes commensurate with what they regard as their status and level of skill, and because those persons are in a position to charge rates that permit them to approach this income goal.

As for the fact that legal services are personal services, it should be recognized that mechanization (and computerization) are not irrelevant to the handling of legal problems. Many transactions can be routinized and organized in such a way that they can ordinarily be handled with a minimum application of discretion or judgment. Transactions such as payments by check, collection of taxes, recording property transfers, insurance and annuities, etc., at one time were done by hand, often the hand of a lawyer. Now they are done mostly by machine, at considerable saving. But many transactions still have to be tailored to the occasion, and it is for these that a lawyer may be brought in.

A lawyer conceives of himself as worth a good wage. The range of lawyers' compensation is very great, running from a high of about $500,000 a year (for a few extraordinarily successful lawyers, many of whom do not work for corporations) to a low of something less than $10,000 for underemployed marginal practitioners. An individual lawyer's income also ranges considerably over his career; lawyers in corporate practice and government service aged 24 or so now receive salaries ranging from about $14,000 to $27,000 and reach a peak in their 50s and early 60s of anywhere from about $45,000 in government service to $75,000 to $300,000 or so in the private sector. Thus, averages are misleading. Nevertheless, the median for the profession as a whole is probably about $30,000 and for lawyers in high grade corporate practice considerably more, probably about $50,000 per year.

The reasons lawyers in this level of practice can command such an income appear to be fairly simple. First, their skills are easily transferable to vocations where the compensation is at about these levels, when account is taken of such factors as fringe benefits, security, autonomy, etc. This is because the lawyer for a corporation or government agency is, among other things, an all-purpose bureaucrat. He can move into business entrepreneurship, corporate management, marketing, finance, public administration, or become a go-between of one sort or another. Many lawyers do make this move, so that attraction out of law practice puts constant pressure on the compensation levels within it. Second, in high level law practice relatively small differences in competence can make a substantial difference in the results achieved for a client, just as small differences in ability make a big difference in result in competitive sports. This means that in the areas where differences in result have large consequences, as they do in the affairs of big businesses, the premium for the marginally superior performer is very great.

Paying a staff of lawyers an average annual salary of $50,000 translates into standard rates ranging from $50 to

$150 per hour and averaging about $75 per hour, allowing for overhead. At these rates, middle and lower income people simply cannot afford legal services except to protect interests they prize very highly, such as staying out of jail or getting compensation for serious personal injury. But such people are not the only ones to whom the cost of lawyers' fees is burdensome. Even large corporate clients feel pillaged by legal fees that accumulate at this rate. Corporate clients sometimes attribute the cost to the lawyer who bills them, but more often to the government regulations that made the services necessary in the first place. Perhaps they and other users of legal services are always possessed by a sometimes unrecognized source of indignation: If the lawyer gets a bad result for his client, the fee adds injury to injury; if he gets a good result, the fact that his high-priced services were necessary to the vindication of justice adds injury to insult.

Corporate clients have adapted to the cost of legal services by trying to reorganize the way they meet their legal needs. It is the pressure of cost, indeed, that explains the emergence of "in house" legal departments in corporations and government agencies, for originally all legal services were rendered by independent practitioners.

In this connection it is useful to make a comparison between the corporate legal department and the independent law firm. In terms that exaggerate the difference for purposes of explanation, it goes something like this: An independent law firm is organized to deal intensively and on short notice with relatively complex and novel legal problems whose resolution requires a large element of judgment, assertiveness, and composure under stress. It has rapidly expansible capacity, which means professionals willing to work all hours for weeks on end and a large supporting cast of paraprofessionals. All these capabilities add greatly to the cost of the service. A corporate law department, on the other hand, is organized to deal systematically with a continuous stream of transactions to make sure that they are "debugged" from a legal viewpoint. It is responsible for seeing that abnormal situations are isolated for special attention, at higher echelons in the legal department or by referral to independent counsel. Furthermore, a considerable amount of the effort of a corporate legal department goes into devising procedures for use by the client's administrative bureaucracy that will even more fully simplify and standardize its transactions. The aim is to assure that as many transactions as possible can be routinely handled without referral for legal attention. In short, the independent firm partakes of the character of a group of free-lance professionals while the corporate law department or government law department partakes of the character of a properly trained civil service.

To minimize its cost for legal services, the corporation or government agency must sort out its legal affairs so that most of them can be handled by the relatively less expensive processes of the legal department and the nonlegal administrative offices of the client. A corporate client has an incentive to do this in a purely rational way. It requires honest advice from its legal advisers, inside and outside, as to what tasks can safely be assigned to administrative staff rather than outside counsel. There is, of course, risk that the advice may be distorted by self-interest, just as a lawyer for an individual can suggest more expensive legal procedures than the client really needs. In this respect, the corporate client like the individual client is at the mercy of his lawyer's integrity. The corporate client's risk in the long run is less than an individual user of legal services, however, because its need for repeated services results in its becoming informed and sophisticated about the price of what it buys.

The task of a government agency in cost minimization is substantially the same as that of a corporation. However, there is reason to think that the government's approach to cost accounting for legal services is probably less acute than that of a business corporation. This is because it is very difficult to determine precisely what a government agency is responsible for achieving (it has no counterpart of a profit and loss statement), and therefore what are gains and losses. This in turn makes it difficult to say for a government agency what are efficient means of maximizing gain and minimizing loss. Rather than engineer its services to its needs, a government agency generally perforce proceeds in a reverse fashion. The agency establishes a service, such as a legal department, and then adapts use of the service to the capacity of the staff. This results in most all of its legal transactions (except extraordinary ones such as the Watergate Special Prosecutor) being handled in the style of a properly trained civil service. Accordingly, except when it employs special counsel, the government is never victimized by excessive fee rates. On the other hand, it may be chronically victimized by making use of journeymen professionals when it needs the services of masters. One of the Seven Springs participants complained how much it had cost the government to retain private counsel. (The cases involved employees so situated that conflict of interest made it improper for regular government legal staff to represent them.) The question could equally well be asked whether the government had simply gotten used to paying too little, and getting a corresponding quality of service.

In this perspective, concern on the part of clients about excessive legal fees is in many respects warranted but almost always misdirected. If the legal services to be purchased are hand-tailored to individual situations, they will be expensive for the same reason that surgery, portraiture, custom haberdashery, and haute cuisine are expensive. If legal services can be purchased in a form that is standardized, they can be made cheaper, for the same reason that fluoride dental therapy, rack suits, and McDonald's hamburgers are inexpensive. This does not mean that the costs corporations incur for legal services are not substantial. On the contrary, they are large and are rising as regulation of their activities becomes more exacting. It means only that the large business corporation, as a sophisticated purchaser in the legal services market, has been able to service its legal needs with a mix of service arrangements adapted to its mix of legal needs.

The fee problem so far as the average citizen is concerned is that the rules laid down by the legal profession, concerning how legal services may be supplied, do not give him that choice. He is not allowed to obtain legal services from banks or real estate brokers or divorce counselling agencies, even if the services are provided by a licensed lawyer. He is not allowed to obtain legal services from law firms that could combine mass production with advertising, though this prohibition has now been undercut to some extent by the U. S. Supreme Court. It is the position of the legal profession that these restrictions serve the public interest by providing protection against unscrupulous practitioners.

The question is of no direct concern to the elite corporate practitioner. Elite firms render services to ordinary individuals only if the problems involve a lot of money or when the matter is going to be billed at reduced fee or as legal aid. The question is of very deep concern to economically marginal practitioners, however, for they are most vulnerable to changes in the rules that would permit streamlining of legal services. The question at issue is a different order of ethical problem than that concerning whether the fee charged an individual in a specific instance was excessive. This is why public concern about lawyers' fees is misdirected. Possibly it is why most of the bar does not see the question as an ethical problem at all.

8. The Revolving Door

It is recurrently asserted that a lawyer employed by the government should not be allowed to enter private practice involving the kinds of things he did while in government service. It is also often questioned whether a government agency should employ a lawyer from private practice who has represented clients that are subject to the agency's jurisdiction. These are aspects of a personnel practice of long standing sometimes called the "revolving door."

Many lawyers who work for the government, particularly the federal government, in time leave to join private law firms. Young lawyers often begin their careers with the government because the government pays competitive salaries at lower position levels and gives their incumbents far greater responsibilities than those entrusted to professionals of comparable age and experience in the private sector. The careers of many experienced lawyers—those in their 30s and 40s—are often punctuated with a term of high level service in the government, at least if the tide of political fortune coincides with their own inclinations and availability. A stint in Washington, or at the cabinet level of state government, provides an experienced lawyer opportunity to do some interesting things he cannot do in private practice—make public policy, participate openly in political power struggles, and be rid of his clients for a while. And a few lawyers become statesmen, returning in their senior years to help run the government and make history.

So far as it involves experienced lawyers, this pattern is not new. At the highest levels of appointment, it is a concomitant of electoral politics. In an elective system, policy makers by definition hold office on a temporary basis, being subject to ouster when the mandate changes. With regard to lower level appointments, what has been called the revolving door has an historical antecedent in the system of political patronage, which supplied not only warm places near the fire for the party's faithful subalterns but also professional positions, particularly in law. In the present day, those who circulate in and out of government, whether neophytes or seasoned professionals, include economists, scientists, and managers.

The practice has persisted despite recurrent attacks on its legitimacy and integrity. It has been defended on inconsistent grounds. Those who accepted the patronage system have asserted that government jobs were such that almost anyone could do them and hence nothing was lost by having them done by friends of the regime. (The validity of this theory is implicitly reaffirmed by some of the appointments of every new administration.) Reformers of all political persuasions assert that government jobs at the professional level entail such broad discretionary powers that only professionals sympathetic to the elected administration can be entrusted to hold them. Indeed, it can be argued that political-professionals are as necessary to the effectiveness of the presidential system of administration as political-ministers are necessary in a cabinet system. Whether this theory has validity is perhaps arguable. What is important, however, is that the theory is believed to have validity. In any event, experienced professionals are attracted to upper and near-upper echelon positions in part by the prospect of accomplishing something; younger ones are attracted to lower level positions by the prospect of demonstrating professional precocity.

The problem is whether the system involves conflicts of interest that should be regarded as unethical and, if so, what should be done about them. A further problem is whether lawyers who move in and out of government stand in any different position from other kinds of professionals, such as technical people who are associated with defense production or the regulated industries.

There are legal controls on the revolving door. Although the precise terms of the rules have varied and will no doubt be revised in the future, they are of two basic types. One is a rule that a government employee upon leaving government service may not be employed for a specified period by a private company that sold goods or services to the department with which the employee was associated. This kind of rule most often affects professionals who in the private sector have salaried positions with suppliers of hard- and software to the government. The other is a rule that a former government employee may not involve himself on behalf of a private employer in any matter for which he had responsibility while in government service. This type of rule most often affects professionals such as lawyers, who in the private sector are typically engaged in consultative or advisory practice.

It is common ground that a lawyer who has acted for the government in a matter may not upon leaving the government represent a private party in the same matter. It does not make any difference that the positions of the government and the subsequent client appear wholly compatible. Thus, a lawyer who has prosecuted a government antitrust action cannot upon leaving the government represent a private party allegedly injured by the conduct in question. Even in this situation there is potential incompatibility between the interests of the government and the private client. It is in the private client's interest that a government suit be pressed to conclusion, so that the defendant's liability is established, while from the government's viewpoint the suit is only one of many that compete for attention. The risk is that the government's prosecutorial effort would be deflected to benefit the prosectuor's prospective private client. Still more clearly would it be improper for a former government lawyer to represent a private client having an antagonistic interest in a matter for which the lawyer was previously responsible.

The difficult problems are more subtle. One of these concerns the definition of "a matter." It is easy enough to identify the subject of the government lawyer's professional work when one is talking about a lawsuit or a contract negotiation. But what about development of policy or regulations that affect a whole industry, or drafting and lobbying an administration's legislative program? There are also problems of duration of responsibility. Is a legal draftsman of defense procurement regulations barred from ever representing a defense contractor as long as those regulations are still in effect?

The concept of "a matter" is similarly complicated when the subject concerns the responsibilities of a lawyer serving as an agency's general counsel or in a cabinet or subcabinet administrative position. Such an officer is in some sense involved in every transaction of his agency during his tenure. Does it follow that he may not thereafter properly represent any private client in a transaction that was within the agency's jurisdiction in that period? The answer might well be that he should be so disqualified. However, if this is the proper answer, and if it is also true that a lower echelon legal draftsman should not be permanently disqualified from dealing with the subject of his draftsmanship, distinctions have to be drawn between types of involvement for purposes of future disqualification. Drawing such distinctions is not easy, given that the types of involvement run from being attorney general to being a research assistant who sometimes is given a chance to carry another lawyer's briefcase.

Another dimension to the problem arises from the principle of imputation. The principle is that a lawyer's relationship to a client is imputed to his professional associates and hence determines their disqualifications as well. Thus, if a lawyer has represented the government in a matter, and then leaves the government to join a law firm, that firm cannot thereafter represent a private client in that matter, for the disqualification of the lawyer should extend to the other lawyers in his firm. But as applied in the stages of next remove, the principle of imputation can have broad sweep. In one direction, there can be imputation among the lawyers working for a single government agency. For example, a lawyer for an antitrust agency who works on a case against company A may have close working relations with another lawyer in the same agency who is in charge of a case against company B; under a principle of imputation, the first lawyer would be disqualified from subsequently representing not only company A but also company B. In the other direction, if the first lawyer were to join a private firm, not only would all those associated with that firm be disqualified from representing company A, but, if double imputation is applied, the firm is also disqualified from representing company B. Finally, if application of the principle is pushed to the next degree, it follows that any other lawyer associated with the firm when the exgovernment lawyer joined it would carry the disqualification with him, like an infectious disease. If such a lawyer then left the firm and joined another, the latter would also be disqualified from representing company A. There is no logical stopping place, only a practical one.

The impact of the disqualification rule, especially when applied with its imputation corollary, can be very severe for a lawyer who has neither an independent income nor an academic base to return to. A lawyer who has held a high level position may have to reenter practice as a solo practitioner, lest he contaminate a whole firm. Former Attorney General Herbert Brownell followed this course after his service in the Eisenhower administration, for example. Although such a solution seems extreme, it apparently does not deter senior lawyers from serving the government in high office. Not only are the responsibilities and prestige of high office a compelling inducement in themselves, but the lawyers eligible for these positions have sufficient professional stature that they could make a living even if their practice were limited to purely nongovernment transactions. But the problem is quite different for lawyers considering government service at a somewhat lower level and for newly admitted law graduates who might seek a position with the government as their first job.

If the rule of disqualification were rigorously applied, younger lawyers would have to consider that service with the government might entail severely restricted reentry into the private professional market. Setting up a solo practice or forming a new firm is generally not a realistic alternative for a lawyer who has no well established position in the private market. Only a few can find their way into the academic world and not all of them would want to follow that path. To be sure, employment can be found in some other line of work but that would involve at least temporary retirement from the profession. Thus, the suitable alternative employment for a lawyer working for the government is a law firm, preferably one with a practice involving the government. Unless there is leeway in application of the disqualification rule, however, that alternative is closed and the attractiveness of government professional employment thereby diminished.

Leeway has been provided through the practice of waiver of the disqualification. The waiver procedure assumes the existence of a broad rule of disqualification, so that all former government lawyers are prima facie debarred from anything having to do with their previous work with the government. However, upon a disclosure of the intended practice affiliation, waiver is then sought from the government with such specific limitations on clientele as seem fitting in the circumstances. Under current practice, waiver is routinely granted on these terms. The procedure parallels that used for dealing with conflict of interest among private clients—consent of the client after full disclosure.

Another proposal for dealing with the problem is "walling off." The idea is that the firm could still represent a client after the former government lawyer joined it, even in matters in which he had participated while in government, but that he would be "walled off" from the firm's work for that client. As an arrangement for handling specific situations, the idea is no different from the waiver procedure. As an arrangement to be adopted as a general rule, it seems to be the epitome of naive legalism. No one who is anxious about the fidelity of former government lawyers will regard such a rule as adequate; and everyone who thinks the problem is primarily one of an individual's trustworthiness will regard the rule as obnoxious. "Walling off" is thus like the alleged New England practice of bundling, having neither the credibility of real prophylaxis nor the dignity of real self-control.

Recently, a movement has been initiated to terminate the wavier procedure. The argument is that the wavier procedure cannot be impartially administered. This is because the waiver procedure is administered by the lawyers still in the government, and they are predisposed to administer it liberally because they want to keep the professional exits open for themselves. The proposal to abolish the waiver procedure has been forestalled at least temporarily, but if nothing else it has rekindled debate about the propriety of revolving door law practice for the government.

As many lawyers familiar with the Washington scene have said, abolition of the wavier procedure would make it much more difficult for the government to attract young lawyers of high competence and would have some adverse effect on recruitment of upper echelon professionals. The government would not have difficulty finding bodies to fill its positions and might actually come out ahead in middle range positions, where career service government lawyers now suffer the frustration of being passed over in favor of outsiders. But the range of competence is very great among lawyers having the same formal qualifications and the government service in general does not offer incentives, certainly not in money and often not in responsibility, to hold able people in the face of private market blandishment. If the available choices were life-time government service or private practice, government service is unlikely to fare well among really competent professionals. Reduction of mobility in and out of the government would therefore probably cost the government a good deal in terms of the technical proficiency of its legal staff.

If the problem is looked at in longer term perspective, the implications of eliminating easy mobility in and out of government seem more complex. As a point of beginning it can be said that if the government were regarded as simply another client, serving it with revolving door lawyers would simply not be countenanced. One cannot imagine a multinational corporation maintaining a legal staff headed by the former counsel of one of its chief competitors and comprised of juniors bound in a few years to join the service of other competitors. A professional personnel policy that is at least arguably desirable for the government is thus unarguably undesirable for a private enterprise. This might suggest that the government should obviously stop the revolving door. But equally it suggests that there may be unexplored reasons that make it inappropriate to treat the government like a private enterprise in this respect.

One way to explore these reasons is to describe a model of a government legal staff governed by a rigid restriction on "revolving." The rule could be that a lawyer who left the government could not for three years appear before the agency in which he served and could not be associated with a client who had a matter before the agency during the lawyer's tenure.

For practical purposes this would mean that a lawyer leaving government would have to pursue a practice in some other area of law than the one in which he was involved when in the government. For very young lawyers, those in the first two years or so of practice, this would not be much of a burden. The elementary skills mastered in this phase of professional development—researching, writing, speaking, dealing effectively with opposite numbers—are readily transferable to other types of practice. Beyond this apprenticeship stage, however, the lawyer becomes a specialist in whatever he is doing, particularly if he is employed by a client with problems such as a government agency. Specialization involves more than mastery of the present law in a subject. It also involves the mastery of the subject's history and politics, the structure of power in which it is administered, and the character and abilities of the principal players in the field. That kind of knowledge is not readily transferable to other fields and becomes rapidly obsolete. A lawyer leaving the government after five or six years of service with an agency would therefore have to abandon the most valuable part of his intellectual capital, unless he was one of the few who could sell it in the academic market place.

A lawyer entering government service at the beginning of his career would thus have to plan an exit after three or four years, or anticipate then having to decide to stay on for the rest of his professional life. A lawyer entering government service after his apprenticeship would have to assume he was committing himself to a more or less permanent career change.

If this schema is correct, the government's legal staff under the regime of a strict limitation on mobility would have a somewhat different composition than it has now. It would be essentially a career service, occasionally augmented by visiting professors. The middle echelons and above would be career staff because individuals having reached that level could not afford to leave for private practice. Private practitioners could make lateral entry into the system only on a permanent basis, and even that kind of movement would probably be eliminated by political pressure from the permanent staff to require that its members be given preference in all higher position openings. The government would no longer be an atractive first employer for young lawyers who wanted positions of responsibility, because reaching those positions would lock them out of the private sector. The government could not afford to hire youngsters merely for an apprenticeship, however, and so would discourage terms of service that were less than three years. As a result, most of those entering at the bottom would be intent upon making government service a career.

In this scenario, cabinet level officers presumably would change with administrations. Below this, however, and certainly in offices of agency general counsel, there would be relatively little of the infiltration from the private sector that is now characteristic of government service. The staff would resemble the legal departments of some large corporations and the core of the legal staffs of most government agencies. It would replicate the legal departments of most European governments and those of state and local governments in this country that have civil service systems.

It is not at all clear that such an arrangement would be better than what we have now. It would eliminate the most commonly voiced objection to revolving door service, that of conflicts of interest. It would end the valuable on-the-job training now afforded by government employment. (What critics of the present system may find most galling is that a professional in temporary service gets advanced training at government expense.) It would result in a staff that would be strong in department expertise, in loyalty to the agency and the government generally, in personal probity, and in bureaucratic street wisdom.

Possibly such a system would be preferable to a purely patronage system on the model attributed to President Jackson. But it would have limitations of its own. Staff would be composed of people preferring a government career to the viscissitudes of the private sector, and therefore on the average likely to be more conservative, more cautious, and more "technical" than their legal counterparts in the private sector. The ties of the legal staff to the agency would be more intimate and would involve less self-criticism. Dependency on the pleasure of Congress would be greater and hence also the susceptibility to legislative pressure. The policy of an agency so staffed could not be redirected by infiltration of operating personnel but through the much more difficult procedure of orders from above or outside. In short, the legal departments of government in general might well look like those of, say, the Corps of Engineers and the Food and Drug Administration, rather than the Justice Department or the Securities and Exchange Commission.

If this analysis of the purist alternative is anywhere near accurate, the conclusion can be drawn that it leaves a lot to be desired from the viewpoint of the government. A career staff lawyer is a lawyer who has only one client all of his professional life. Lawyers with such a background necessarily lack the professional range of a more heterogeneous staff. They are more isolated from the professional fraternity, for whatever that might be worth. Perhaps most important, their definition of loyalty to client could well be of a kind that is not an unalloyed virtue, for proper loyalty to the client is modified by obligations to others and faithfulness to some external mandate that we may call professional duty. What seems clear is that real sensitivity to these conflicts is the product of experiencing them, repeatedly and in endlessly varying form. Putting aside all other questions, it is difficult to believe that government career staff would have equivalent opportunity to share that experience.

As things now stand, government legal staffs are a mixture of political appointments at the top, career people in the middle, and younger people of unresolved ambition at the bottom. It would be a mistake to assume that this arrangement is perfect in balance though fortuitous in origin. Of course, one could hope for a more fundamental change. One could hope that government service, not only in law but in other disciplines, could be made so attractive that the professionals of highest ability would be drawn into government careers. Doing so would require the professionals to be given higher salaries, greater autonomy (especially from the influence of Congress), and distinct identity—endowments now provided only to the federal judiciary, the Foreign Service, the military, and perhaps a few other government establishments. This would make government professionals in law much like their counterparts in a Ministry of Justice in the European model or the Civil Service in Britain, an elite not beholden to the marketplace or to partisan politics.

The gains to be had in such a service could be substantial, but the possibility of its being established in this country seem remote. The public attitude toward high pay and high status for public officials is not sympathetic, to put it mildly. Perhaps critics of the present situation have in mind a service made up of dedicates like Ralph Nader; but that is a style that few people seem to sustain after age 35. It seems more realistic to expect that the choice is between something like the present revolving door system and one in which the government legal service is composed essentially of professional technicians, with both positive and negative connotations of that term. Given that we expect government agencies to originate policy as well as to execute it, and given that policy making is strongly influenced by legal staff, the present system may well be superior. At any rate, it would be a mistake to assume that private lawyers now usually enter government so that they can fix things for their clients. And it surely cannot be all bad that, under the present system, many members of the private bar at one time have had the responsibility for enforcing the law.

9. The Adversary System

The adversary system is a procedure for trial of civil and criminal cases, and is the characteristic form of trial procedure in common law countries. Its essential feature is that a decision is made by judge, or judge with jury, who finds the facts and determines the law from submissions made by partisan advocates on behalf of the parties. The system contrasts with what is generally called the inquisitorial system, used in countries of the civil law tradition such as France and Germany. In this system of trial, which might less invidiously be called the interrogative system, the judge determines the law and finds the facts by his own active investigation and inquiries at trial.

There is probably no "pure" form of either system. Even the most passive judge in an adversary system sometimes asks questions and even the most passive litigant in an interrogative system is something of an advocate when he gives his responses. Furthermore, there are different forms of adversary procedures that vary in the contentiousness of their mood, as interrogative procedures also vary in the intensity with which inquiry is pursued. Nevertheless, the adversary system is distinctive for the fact that the parties, through their lawyers, investigate the facts, frame the legal issues, and present the evidence to a passive tribunal that then reaches decision.

The adversary system has deep roots in the Anglo-American legal tradition. Its antecedent is often said to be the Norman trial by battle, wherein issues in doubt were resolved by the outcome of a duel. Perhaps more relevant is the fact that the key elements of the adversary system—the right to present

THE ADVERSARY SYSTEM 121

evidence and the right to assistance of counsel—evolved as legal controls on government absolutism in seventeenth-century England. Thus, the adversary system is not only a theory of adjudication but a constituent of our history of political liberty.

The theory of adjudication in the adversary system, as usually stated, has two linked components. One is that party presentation will result in the best presentation, because each party is propelled into maximum effort in investigation and presentation by the prospect of victory; in contrast, a judge-interrogator is only interested in getting through the day and through his caseload. The other component of the theory is more complex and has to do with the psychology of decision making. It runs essentially as follows: Proof through evidence requires hypothesis; hypothesis requires a preliminary mind-set; if an active judge-interrogator develops the proof, his preliminary mind-set too easily can become his final decision; therefore, it is better to have conflicting preliminary hypotheses and supporting proofs presented by the parties so that the judge's mind can be kept open until all the evidence is at hand.

In this version of the adversary theory, the role of the advocate is central to adjudication, because the advocate is a necessary orchestrator of the proof to be offered by a party. The prominence of the advocate in the adversary system explains in part why the legal profession as a whole strongly supports it. There are other interpretations of the adversary system, however, that attach much less significance to the role of the advocate as an instrument for developing the proofs. One of these interpretations emphasizes the importance of party participation, the idea being that a party's presentation of the case on his behalf gives him a sense of involvement and control in the decision procedure. In this conception of the adversary system, counsel is and should be relegated to the role of coach rather than protagonist, because if the lawyer is protagonist, his client's role is secondary and passive. This form of the adversary system appears to have actually existed in English procedure of about the thirteenth century, but it is found today only in cases, such as in small claims court, where the amount involved is too little to justify hiring a lawyer to present them. These days, if litigation is taken to a lawyer, he takes it over.

There is still another and more radical theory of the adversary system. On this view, trials are not quests for truth in a serious objective or empirical sense, and cannot be. This is because truth is unknowable in any objective sense, or at least because the controversies in which the issues can rationally be resolved by the evidence rarely go to trial, for parties concede what can really be proved. By exclusion, therefore, in the cases that go to trial the evidence is hopelessly ambiguous according to any concept of rational proof, and decision necessarily involves important elements of intuition, predisposition, and bias. On this analysis, a trial is necesarily theatre or ritual to an important extent.

The adversary system has a strange status in the Americn legal tradition. As noted earlier, it is one derivative of fundamental theories of political liberty. Great cases in the adversary tradition are part of our constitutional folklore—Andrew Hamilton's defense of John Peter Zenger, John Adams's defense of the British soldiers in the Boston Massacre, the Scottsboro case, etc. In recent years, the Supreme Court has substantially equated adversarial trial with due process in the determination of legal rights. Furthermore, the notion that adjudication should proceed by means of competitive presentation has a strong philosophical affinity with the idea of freedom in science, letters, and the arts. As freedom in those domains inheres in open competition in the "marketplace of ideas," so there is freedom in adjudication when it consists of open competition in presentation of evidence and argument. In these respects, the adversary system stands with freedom of speech and the right of assembly as a pillar of our constitutional system. On the other hand, the adversary system in practice is known by its practitioners often to be anything but the truth-revealing process that it pretends to be. When brought forward for discussion at Seven Springs, it was thoroughly savaged.

The discussion was initiated by consideration of a thesis previously developed by one of the participants, Judge Marvin Frankel.[1] In essence, the thesis is that an advocate should have a responsibility not merely to present evidence favorable to his client, and to counter unfavorable evidence, but also should share with the judge the responsibility for getting at the truth. As this thesis was explored in the discussion, the following observations were made about the adversary system as it currently exists:

— It is expensive and unwieldy. Its use would be abandoned but for the fact that most cases are not actually tried, the civil cases being mostly settled and the criminal cases being mostly disposed of by bargained plea.
— It involves systematic distortion of the truth. Perjured evidence is commonplace in criminal cases and more than occasional in civil cases, and reconstruction of witness recollection is standard technique. Questioning is conducted not to enlighten but to entrap. Procedural technicality is routinely exploited to impose delay and expense on opposing parties. The procedure for pretrial discovery of evidence is an engine of harassment, having in effect put blank search warrants at the litigants' disposal.

---

1. Frankel, "The Search for Truth: An Umperial View," 123 *U. Penna. L. Rev.* 1031 (1975).

— In cases having public policy significance, the courtroom often is converted into an adjunct political forum in which judicial procedure is used as a device of interest-group warfare. Major antitrust, environmental, civil rights, and some kinds of criminal cases frequently undergo this transformation.
— In criminal cases, the procedure is often a complete charade. For example, a guilty defendant can suppress evidence on the ground that it was obtained in violation of the rules governing police investigations, only to be found guilty on the basis of police agent testimony fabricated to offset the effects of the suppression.
— The public views the whole process with cynical abhorrence.
— Lawyers, at least ones not specialists in trial work, regard a trial as an unmitigated evil, to be avoided if possible but otherwise to be fought according to the prevailing conventions.

As the discussion developed, a pall descended on the participants. Some hopeful suggestions were advanced, but desultorily or with irony:

— Maybe arbitration is better; it is cheaper, faster, more private, and less arbitrary. But there was not much optimism about it. The bar at large would be against arbitration as a substitute for adjudication, and would fly the flag and play the national anthem to sustain a successful opposition. Lawyers with experience in arbitration thought that arbitrators were inclined to split the difference between parties, whatever it was, and would not be tough with an obstructionist party.
— Maybe the adversary system would be satisfactory if there were no jury. But abolishing the jury system would require constitutional change that is practically impossible. Furthermore, in the participants' view many of the judges are

THE ADVERSARY SYSTEM

not much better; at least with a jury there is always a chance of getting someone who is reasonably concerned, intelligent, and disinterested.
— There are good versions of the adversary system. A trial before a capable federal judge presented by competent counsel is a fair trial. But this doesn't happen very often.
— Just results can often be achieved when the judges are simply terrible. Litigants confronted by the ordeal of trial before a judge who is an idiot or bigot will quickly compose their differences — the Quasimodo technique of justice.
— Perhaps all advocates should be governed by the standards applicable to prosecutors. A prosecutor is supposed to be not only a partisan advocate but also a minister of justice, responsible for seeing that unjustified prosecutions are not brought and unjustified convictions not obtained. Why should not all attorneys have such a responsibility?

At this point, the following discussion ensued:

— The prosecutor is unique because he does not have a specific client to and for whom he is responsible. If you have a client, you have to represent him and not "justice" in some abstract sense.
— Well then, why must the advocate in an adversary system be responsible to his client in the way to which we have become accustomed? Why could the advocate not, at least in criminal cases, be a member of the court's staff, responsible to the court for investigating and presenting the side to which he is assigned? Wouldn't that reproduce the functional elements of the present adversary system without its redundancies and excesses?
— There is much to be said for such a system. Indeed, it embodies substantially the theory and practice of the system of adjudication used in the countries that describe themselves as socialist, meaning not only the Soviet Union

but also such less patently autocratic regimes as that in Yugoslavia. That, of course, is not a reason for rejecting a reformation in favor of such a system, but it is perhaps a reason for carefully reflecting upon the desirability of doing so.

— The suggestion seems to be that, although the attachment of advocate to client begets the perversions we have been talking about, the detachment of advocate from client might beget worse.

On that note of resignation, the discussion died out. It was revived only briefly to deal with an issue that has long agitated both the bar and its critics. This is whether an advocate should be allowed to aid his client in presenting testimony that the advocate knows to be false.

Specifically the problem is this: An advocate has a duty not to present false evidence, but he also has a duty not to conduct himself so as to prejudice his client. In civil cases, it is generally accepted that the advocate should never present false evidence and that he has a duty to see that his client produces evidence legitimately demanded by the other side, even if the evidence is very damaging. In criminal cases, it is recognized that the prosecutor has a duty as minister of justice to prevent the use of fabricated evidence against an accused. The unsettled question is whether a lawyer defending a criminal may properly put his client on the stand even when satisfied that the testimony will be perjured. The rules as they stand clearly prohibit the lawyer from doing so. However, most criminal defense lawyers feel this is wrong and many of them actually believe the rule is otherwise; they think the advocate's duty to his client implies that in a criminal case he should conduct the defendant in his testimony even when counsel knows the defendant is lying.[2]

This issue poses in special form a general question for the adversary system: How can a procedure be justified as best

THE ADVERSARY SYSTEM

able to yield truth when certain critical maneuvers in the procedure have the purpose and effect of suppressing the truth? This is an old question. The given answer is that society, and therefore the law, values other things in addition to truth. The problem of priorities is posed in other legal contexts as well, for example:

— Should there be a right of privacy for one's person, papers, and effects even if it means blocking access to the truth? What about compulsory fingerprinting, blood tests, and voice-prints?
— Should people be required to keep records to their transactions, for example to establish the extent of their tax liability? Even if the records are incriminating?
— Should there be an attorney-client privilege?

No question of legal ethics is more difficult than the question whether an advocate can help suppress the truth in order to protect his client. In so far as litigation is concerned,

---

2. On what the rules are and what they are sometimes understood to be, see Rotunda, Book Review (of Freedman, *Lawyers' Ethics in an Adversary System*, 1975), 89 *Harv. L. Rev.* 622 (1976). See also Levine, "Litigation Ethics: Struggling with Ethical Standards in Massachusetts," 3 *Litigation* 43 (1976) (indicating that lawyers differentiate between allowing a defendant to perjure himself and putting on someone else as a witness in his support). See also Battle, "In Search of the Adversary System," 50 *Tex. L. Rev.* 60 (1971). The official position of the bar is that a lawyer may not put his client on the stand when he is convinced the testimony will be perjured. See A.B.A., *Standards of Criminal Justice*, "Standards Relating to the Defense Function," Section 7.7, Commentary. See also Callan and David, "Professional Responsibility and the Duty of Confidentiality: Disclosure of Client Misconduct in an Adversary System," 29 *Rut. L. Rev.* 332 (1976).

the effect is to immobilize the law's enforcement. A lawyer can, within the limits of the law, obstruct its enforcement by advising his client to refuse to testify. At the borderland of the law, and without much risk to himself, he can go a considerable way in helping his client build a coverup. For example, he can advise the client about the consequences of preserving records or indicate to him the legal consequences of a certain line of testimony that the client might give. To the extent that such advice is given and acted upon, the effect is much the same as putting a client on the stand when it is known that his testimony will be false: The truth of the matter, which might have been discovered if the lawyer had not been involved, will less likely be discovered because he is involved. The problem is whether the benefits are worth that cost.

Paradoxically, the primary benefit of the system is often said to be the promotion of truth. For every instance in which truth is suppressed or distorted by the adversary system, it is thought there are more instances in which the system uncovers truth that otherwise would not have been uncovered. There is no practicable way to test this claim. It is worth considering, however, whether the situation would really be much better if we gave up the adversary system in favor of the interrogative system. But even if the claim were false we might want to keep the rule as it is. Under the present system, using ostensibly open competition for discovery of the truth, the law has troubles with suppression and distortion; what sort of troubles would it have if we depended on *ex officio* procedures for getting the evidenc? If the truth suffers from our use of the adversary system, we ought to consider how it might suffer if we used some other system. In our political culture, the interrogative system of trial could well turn out to resemble Congressional hearings.

THE ADVERSARY SYSTEM

The real value of the adversary system thus may not be its contribution to truth but its contribution to the ideal of individual autonomy. This is the rationale underlying many rules that obscure the truth, such as the privilege against self-incrimination and the rule that private premises may not be searched without a warrant. The proposition, as applied to the adversary system, is that there is good in being able to say what one wants to say, even if it involves the commission of perjury. Stated baldly, the proposition is shocking. The norms of our society condemn lying, although it is perhaps worth noting that the biblical rule is the much narrower proposition that one should not bear false witness against a neighbor. At any rate, conventional morality does not openly recognize the value of being able to lie. Still, our commitment to truthfulness may actually go no further than homily; when it comes to serious beusiness such as negotiation and diplomacy, most people accept the utility, the inevitability, and perhaps even the desirability of dissimulation in various forms.

Why should dissimulation not be acceptable in court? There are many cultures in which it is assumed that parties to legal conflict lie on their own behalf; no pretense is made that they should be expected to do otherwise. The common law formerly exhibited the same attitude, for it did not allow testimony from a criminal defendant or any "party in interest" in civil litigation. The present ethical dilemma in the adversary system may therefore be ultimately traceable to the abolition of the common law rules of witness disqualification.

The reform of the common law rules occurred in the nineteenth century. It was based on the proposition that few injustices would result if interested persons were allowed to testify. It was believed that with cross-examination and the good sense of the jury, the truth will out most of the time.

Perhaps it is time that this premise was reexamined, for it seems evident that if the stakes involved in a lawsuit are substantial, if the outcome depends on the truth, and if the parties are authorized to give evidence as to what the truth is, the parties will distort their submissions to the maximum extent possible. The artistry and self-consciousness of the distortion will of course vary. In many cases it may be supposed that at least one party will tell the unvarnished truth, hoping if not trusting that it will be seen as such. But to require a party to choose between imprisonment or financial self-destruction on the one hand, and complete truthfulness on the other, is to impose a moral burden that may simply be too heavy. And, directly to the point of the present discussion, it imposes nearly as difficult a burden on the advocate who must advise the party in making the choice.

There is much ambivalence concerning the advocate's responsibility in this respect. The rules clearly say that, even in the defense of criminal cases, the advocate may not assist his client in committing perjury or in otherwise fabricating or suppressing evidence. In practice, lawyers often wind up violating these rules, some of them quite frequently. But they seek escapes from moral responsibility for having done so.

There are several escapes. It is said that no client is guilty until found so by a court; therefore, one cannot know what the truth is until then; therefore, one cannot conclude that a client's testimony will constitute perjury. This is pure casuistry. Of course there are doubtful situations, but there are also ones that are not doubtful. A thing is not made true or not by a court's pronouncing on it, and a lawyer can reach conclusions about an issue without having a judge tell him what to think.

Another escape is for the advocate to indicate to the client how inconvenient it would be if the evidence were such and so, and leave it to the client to do the dirty work—well

THE ADVERSARY SYSTEM

illustrated in "the lecture" in *Anatomy of a Murder*.[3] Another is for the advocate to pretend that the rules governing his responsibility are different from what they are—to pretend that duty to client requires aiding him in whatever the client feels he must do to vindicate himself in court. The advocate is then absolved because he is merely an instrument.

As the situation stands, the advocate is supposed to be both the champion of his client and a gatekeeper having a duty to prevent his client from contaminating the courtroom. In principle, these responsibilities are compatible. The duty to the court simply limits the ways in which a lawyer can champion his client's cause. In practice, however, the duties have come to be in perhaps uncontrollable conflict.

The sources of this conflict are located in the depths of our system of advocacy. An important factor in the advocate's ability to control the conflict is the set of rules that describe his relationship to the client and the cause. In other legal systems, these relationships are quite different from what they are in this country. In the English system, for example, the barrister is insulated from the case in several important ways. An English barrister has no continuing relation with any client; his fee is fixed before trial in negotiations to which he is not a party and on a basis unrelated to eventual victory or defeat; the case is placed with a barrister through a solicitor as intermediary; and barristers as a group are small in number, aristocratic, clannish, and closely tied to the judiciary. The barrister thus is strongly identified as an officer of the court and as a gatekeeper concerning what kind of evidence will be offered. In the continental system, the advocate is insulated from the client by somewhat similar

---

3. Traver, *Anatomy of a Murder* (1958).

conventions; equally important, he has a much more limited responsibility in the trial because the judge and not the advocate is primarily responsible for eliciting the facts.

In the American system, however, the advocates' relationship to his client's cause is much more dependent and intimate. In litigation involving "repeat business" clients, the advocate or his firm usually is also counsel under retainer to the client. In litigation involving "one shot" clients, such as plaintiff's injury claims, the lawyer's fee is usually contingent on the outcome. In any event, the advocate is expected and permitted to investigate the facts and interrogate witnesses before trial, thus becoming a party to the evidence before its presentation in court. A much wider range of harassing tactics is indulged in American litigation. Hence, the advocate's situation in our version of the adversary system is fairly defined by Shaw's description of marriage: it "combines the maximum of temptation with the maximum of opportunity." It is not difficult to see why the lawyer may be relatively ineffective as a source of restraint on his client.

The advocate who represents large corporations rarely confronts the problems of client perjury or fabrication or destruction of evidence. But he faces problems that are similar if more subtle. What does a lawyer do with the client who wants to fight the case to the bitter end, even though the advocate thinks that the other side's case is substantially just and that the matter should be settled? What does he do in a case where he is convinced that the other side is wrong on the merits but also convinced that the judge or jury or administrative hearing officer will be prejudiced against his corporate client? Does this justify the use of harassing tactics? If the case has a political aspect, may he delay its progress in the hope that there will be a change in administration? If so, within what limits? Legitimate and illegitimate techniques shade into each other—vigorous maneuver into harrassment, careful preparation of witnesses into subornation of perjury, nondisclosure into destruction of evidence. At some point in deterioration of rules of form, an expert in rough and tumble becomes simply a thug. This brings in view another serious problem of the adversary system. The trial lawyer can become completely immersed in his lawsuits, to the point where they become his identity and their outcome the sole criterion of his professional stature. Indeed, it is often only with difficulty that a modern trial specialist can maintain distance between himself and his craft. The whole tendency of his work leads him to hold, with Vince Lombardi, that winning is not the most important thing but the only thing. And the result can be that he becomes incapacitated to give his client detached advice about the prospects of ultimate victory and the advisability of settling through compromise. The problem can be especially severe in "big" cases for and against big corporations, because one such case can for several years be the vocation of a good part of a firm or agency's litigation staff. But it is inherent in the system. An English barrister is reported to have remonstrated, upon the prospect of compromising a bitter suit between heirs to a large fortune, "What? And allow that magnificent estate to be frittered away among the beneficiaries?"

If it is possible that the adversary system can work satisfactorily, and necessary that it must do so because no other system of adjudication is likely to be any better, it remains true that the system in its present form is pretty sick. The problem can be posed in terms of the attitude with which the advocate should approach a case. One approach, whether in reality or in idealized form we cannot be entirely sure, is that of the English barrister. In this approach, the advocate undertakes a dispassionate analysis of the facts and a magisterial consideration of the law with the aim of establishing common ground with his opposite number and thereupon settling the case on the basis of truth and legal justice, or at worst, isolating for trial the issues of fact or law that prove intractable. A lot of litigation in this country is actually determined this way, when the advocates trust each other's competence, integrity, and judgment. But a lot of litigation is conducted otherwise. In the other approach the advocate is a streetfighter—aggressive, guilful, exploitive. Some clients seem to want it that way, at least until they find out that two can play the game. At any rate many clients suppose that is the way litigation inevitably must be conducted and approach their counsel with a corresponding set of expectations. The advocate in turn can confirm and exploit these expectations, providing fulfillment of the prophecy if he wishes. As the institution of adversary adjudication now stands, the advocate has very strong inducements to oblige.

If the adversary system is to be changed, it will not be a simple undertaking. The system as it exists expresses a number of strongly held beliefs and ideals. One is that justice should be free. It is this proposition that supports the rule that the loser in litigation does not have to pay the winner's expenses. From this in turn follows the contingent fee system and the lack of inhibitions on running up an opposing party's costs, with the corresponding impairment of the advocate's gatekeeper function. Another belief is that entry into the legal profession should be relatively democratic. From this proposition it follows that admission is relatively easy, levels of training uneven, and professional esprit de corps weak. From this it follows that the images of professional lawyers are fuzzy and the potential for self-policing correspondingly low. Another is that litigation should secure not only justice under law but natural and popular justice. From this it follows that litigation often has inherently political, redistributive, and sometimes subversive characteristics, which infuse not only the merits of the controversies but the way they are prosecuted or defended. The "Chicago Seven" trial is an illustration. Still another belief is the notion that militant advocacy is an especially genuine and efficacious expression of social conscience. Exemplars of this style are the relentless prosecutor, the fearless vindicator of the oppressed, the wiley strategist for the establishment. It would be better if there were a larger constituency that understood, with Judge Learned Hand, that being in litigation, whatever its outcome, can justly be compared with sickness and death.

Perhaps the problem is this: We can have a system that does not charge user fees, lets everyone play, seeks both law and common justice, and is subject to few inhibitions in style. We can also have a system in which a trial is a serious search for the truth or at least a ceremony whose essential virtue is solemnity. But we probably cannot have both. So long as the advocate in the American system is supposed to be at once a champion in forensic roughhouse and a guardian of the temple of justice, he can fulfill his responsibilities only if he combines extraordinary technical skill with an unusually disciplined sense of probity. That seems to be asking too much of any profession.

10. Advise and Dissent

A client does not always follow his lawyer's adivce on an important matter. So what? Two opposite responses suggest themselves. One is that the client's refusal to follow advice is of no concern to the lawyer, except as it may indicate the advice was wrong and therefore that the lawyer's professional competence may be in question. The other is that the lawyer should terminate his relationship with the client if the matter involves a question of "right and wrong" and the client chooses the wrong course of action. Otherwise, the lawyer would in effect condone wrongdoing by the client—perhaps moral, perhaps legal.

Many courses of action taken by a client are "wrong" at least in the exacting sense that they are not what would be done by a supremely moral person unconcerned with costs. If this were the standard by which a lawyer should judge whether to continue his association with a client, there would be few of either clients or lawyers.

Ethically sensitive lawyers are very much concerned about clients who refuse to follow advice, particularly when it concerns a serious matter of right and wrong. This concern contradicts both the popular lore that the lawyer is simply a tool of this client and the professional dogma that the client's conduct is never morally imputable to his legal adviser. For the skillful lawyer, the question is not what to do if the client refuses to follow advice on an important matter but how to give the advice so that it will not be refused.

In considering this question, it should be kept in mind what a lawyer may include in the advice he gives a client. Legal advice takes the form of a suggestion concerning a course of

ADVISE AND DISSENT

action that might or should be pursued or avoided, with a supporting explanation. The explanation is the heart of the matter, for otherwise the advice amounts to nothing more than a Delphic pronouncement. A legal adviser's explanation can include one or more of the following elements:

— A report of the text of the law as it stands.
— An estimate of how key provisions of the law properly should be interpreted (if the advice is given within the government) or will likely be interpreted by the officials responsible for its administration (if the advice is given outside the government).
— An estimate of the likelihood that a serious effort will be made to invoke the rule in question.
— A projection of the best, worst, and intermediate situations that could result as a consequence of the rule's being invoked.
— An appraisal of the significant consequences of possible courses of action, whether they will provoke retaliation, etc.
— A judgment whether the recommended course of action is in some less pragmatic sense good or right.

The elements of legal advice thus form a spectrum from technicality to morality. It is often impossible to dissever the technical aspect of a legal opinion from the moral and pragmatic considerations that could inform it. What a law "means" depends on the social purposes the law is intended to serve, and these purposes come down to questions of what is good and right. Nevertheless, legal advice can be limited to a report of what the law "is." Of course legal advice can go well beyond such a report.

The rules governing the legal counsellor's role say his ideas of what is good or right may be interjected into his opinion. The Code of Professional Responsibility refers to them as the "those factors which may lead to a decision that is morally just as well as legally permissible." In the affairs of corporations and government agencies, they are more likely to be referred to as "policy considerations." In either event, what is involved are normative standards beyond and presumably above the letter of the law. Similarly, the counsellor may, and with some degree of obligatoriness should, advise the client about the probable interpretation and effects of a rule. As the Code of Professional Responsibility observes, the "lawyer as adviser furthers the interest of his client by giving his professional opinion as to what he believes would likely be the ultimate decision of the courts on the matter at hand and by informing him of the practical effect of such decision."

The rules governing the legal advisor's role thus can be summed up by saying that his advice can comment upon a proposed course of conduct in terms of the letter of the law, its pragmatic implications, and its moral rightness. The question therefore is not what kind of explanation a legal adviser is permitted to give his client when rendering advice; the question is what kind he should give. This depends on what the lawyer seeks to achieve in giving his advice.

The beginning point is that a client is not obliged to follow legal advice, or even to seek it. An attorney-client relationship is not one of tutelage. The client is assumed to be an autonomous person capable of making his or its own decision. He or it is assumed to be responsible for his or its courses of action. The attorney is what is today called a "resouce person," someone who can supply information and advice. He is only one of several kinds of advisor regularly used by a corporation or government agency, along with economists, accountants, scientists, engineers, and clinicians. The same theory applies to their advice: It is information that the client is legally free to ignore in favor of acting according to his own lights.

The attorney whose advice is ignored suffers no legal detriment except possibly that of having to exert greater efforts to collect his fee. He earns his fee even if the advice is rejected, at least as long as it is not so completely wrong as to be worthless. If the advice concerns a course of conduct that would constitute a crime or a fraud, as we have seen the lawyer has an option and perhaps a duty to try to urge the client not to puruse the course of conduct. He may have to report the client's intended behavior to appropriate authorities, although the Code of Professional Responsibility now suggests that this would be an unethical violation of the rule of confidentiality. In any event, the lawyer has the option of resigning from representation of the client. It has been suggested that even this course of action is barred if it would alert law enforcement authorities that the client's activity might be illegal, but only a tortured reading of the rules would sustain such a view. Under extraordinary circumstances, a lawyer may have to resign if he wishes to avoid legal complicity in his client's course of conduct. But the general rule is that the lawyer does not become an accessory before the fact or a joint wrongdoer because he is aware that his client intends a wrongful course of action. In legal contemplation, he is a bystander.

From the client's point of view, the failure to follow legal advice of itself ordinarily has no legal consequences. If the client pursues a course of conduct that his legal advisor has said is illegal or invalid, or generates liability to a third party, there can of course be serious consequences. If it turns out that the advisor was correct, and also that an affected third person or an enforcement agency challenges the course of conduct, the client will suffer whatever follows according to the law. But his liability for such consequences does not ordinarily depend on the fact that he was previously advised about them. The theory is that a person is obliged to conform his conduct to the law. It is ordinarily inadmissible that a person did not specifically know the law; and it is thought to follow, and perhaps does follow, that it is likewise irrelevant that he did specifically know the law but refused to alter his conduct accordingly. Underlying the latter proposition is the idea that a person should not be worse off for having sought legal advice and ignoring it than if he had not sought it at all. On the other hand, there are a few situations—those in which the element of intention is critical—where definite knowledge of the legal status of a course of conduct can make the difference between its being legally wrongful or not.

From the viewpoint of both the client and the legal advisor, then, the theory is essentially that legal advice is delivered on a take it or leave it basis. Underlying this concept is not only the legal idea that the client is autonomous and the attorney a bystander but an image of client and lawyer. The image, here as elsewhere in the professional ethics of the bar, is mid-Victorian. The setting involves two individuals between whom "a matter" is under consideration. Both are adults, both free agents in their respective stations in life; the "matter" is separable in time and space from what has gone before and what may eventuate later. The advice is given and received; the client acts; and that is that.

Given the image, the theory makes sense. In modern setting involving an organizational client, the theory's suitability is no so clear. Organizational clients are not obliged to seek legal advice but they do so as a matter of routine. The routine is supported by several practical necessities. The transactions of large corporations and agencies are generally large in size or frequent in repetition, so that the added cost of obtaining a legal check-out is relatively low. These organizations are relatively vulnerable to legal sactions, especially if the saction of political criticism is included, when they find themselves on the wrong side of legality. The responsible management officials of these organizations may themselves be personally liable, financially or politically, for legally wrongful or invalid actions. Furthermore, when the organization is a government agency, the question of legality is often simultaneously a question of agency jurisdiction and competence. If these considerations do not amount to a legal obligation to seek legal advice, taken together they come close to it.

At the same time, the lawyer for the large organization usually is related to it in such a way that he cannot fairly be called a bystander. There are cases where the mid-Victorian image of detached counsellor still corresponds to reality. An example is the function performed by John McCloy for Gulf Oil Corporation when that company's top management foundered in charges of corruption. He and his firm, not previously having served the company, were brought in as special counsel for the board to investigate whether management had been guilty of misconduct and to advise the board what should be done about it. To some extent, the same detached role is played by a large private firm that advises a corporation only on special occasions, such as big lawsuits, big financings, major regulatory matters, etc. On the other hand, a private firm in a continuous service relationship with a client, as its "general counsel," stands somewhat differently. Even more clearly different is the legal department of a corporation or the counsel's office of a government agency. These law offices are more or less an integral part of the client itself.

The relationship between the general counsel's office and the client can be, and often is, intimate, more so than that between the client and any other staff office. The general counsel's office of a large corporation routinely reviews all major transactions; reports directly to top management or, at least in some circumstances, the board; has connection through its more junior members to lower level echelons of the corporation or agency; is invariably involved in major crises; has a "memory" of earlier crises and vital decisions that usually is at least as complete as that of any office or officer of the company or agency; and has open and accessible communications to outside sources of appraisal, that is, independent legal counsel, to which resort may be had when special objectivity is required. Moreover, the general counsel's office is consulted when legally significant transactions are about to occur, and not merely after they have occurred; it practices mostly preventive law. This significantly affects its position as a giver of advice: An office set up to check the validity of transactions is obviously in a position to reshape ones that would otherwise be plainly illegal. And if special duty does not always follow from special opportunity, it is usually not far behind.

The problem presented in advice giving by such a law office to such a client is therefore rather different from that involved in the Victorian model. First, as a practical matter the client has to seek legal advice and the lawyer has to give it. Second, actually if not in purport, the advice rests upon a different basis of facts than was made available to the lawyer in the Victorian model. The facts on which the modern general counsel's advice is based include not only what the client tells the lawyer on the particular occasion (which would limit the scope of the lawyer's responsibility) but the life history of the client—which the lawyer well knows, perhaps better than the person who sought the advice. Third, the advice is most often addressed to future conduct. For this reason there is a degree of freedom to make the events correspond to whatever standard of conduct might be selected. Fourth, the person who receives the advice will not be acting on his own in deciding whether to follow it; he will act as a company official who is answerable to others if he decides not to follow the advice. Finally, the subject-matter of the advice is an enterprise from which the advisor and person he advises both make a substantial part of their livelihood.

The legal advisor in such a situation surely is not clothed with the immunity of a pure bystander. But what sort of responsibilities does he have? In recent years, some critics of the legal profession have suggested that a lawyer for a corporation is responsible for its conduct in at least two related respects: his advice to such a client should consist not merely of what the client legally might do but also of what the client morally ought to do; and he should not serve a client who is not disposed to follow advice of that character. According to this line of analysis, the probity of a lawyer can be deduced from the conduct of his clients. If the client has engaged in misconduct, his lawyer is prima facie guilty also, either because his advice followed but was morally insufficient, or because his advice was not followed and he has shown himself willing to continue in the service of a morally deficient master. The same analysis could be applied to a lawyer for a government agency.

The attack is a difficult one to meet. The response conventionally made by the bar is to suggest that the same criticism would apply to a lawyer for a criminal accused. If it did, the argument runs, the consequence would be that an accused could not obtain representation by a lawyer of standing; since the latter is inadmissable, it must be that the criticism is invalid. Hence, a lawyer is not responsible for what his client does.

This seems to hold, however, only if the actual relationship between a corporation or agency and its general counsel corresponds to the Victorian model and the latter is limited to criminal cases. It is perfectly possible to think that the lawyer for the criminal accused is not "responsible" for him, while at the same time thinking that the general counsel for a corporation or agency is, in some sense of the word, "responsible" for it. The point is made by suggesting that it is one thing to represent a sometime murderer, quite another to be on retainer to the Mafia.

Thus, the question has to be faced: Is a lawyer responsible for the conduct of a regular client? This is a question that confronts others besides lawyers, a point that has double significance. In the first place, analysis of the lawyer's problem is applicable to other advisers, such as accountants, scientific consultants, and indeed members of the client's own administrative and technical staffs. In the second place, in advising people in important matters the lawyer does not stand in a unique situation. The legal profession often talks as though a legal counsellor bears some special burden because he is privy to especially deep secrets. From this it is thought to follow that he enjoys special immunity from the responsibility that might fall on one who is in some way involved in another's conduct. But the accountant who knows of fraud because he has access to the client's books, or the scientist who knows of poisonous emissions because he has access to the client's premises, is surely in a position that is different at most in degree from a lawyer who has learned of such facts from a consultation with a client.

The obvious answer for the advisor whose advice is ignored is that he can resign. In some circumstances that is the only honorable course to be followed, but it is impractical as a response to all except fundamental disagreements. More important, though not often recognized by the critics of legal and other advisors to corporations, the sanction of resignation involves some ethical problems of its own. If taken seriously, it should be applicable only when any right-thinking advisor would resign. But this is to say that such a client ought to have no right-thinking advisor at all, at least until the client redirects his conduct so that it would no longer be objectionable to a right-thinking advisor. There are situations in which it seems proper that the client should suffer that kind of penalty, for example if he insists on fabricating evidence or carrying out a swindle. But if the case is less extreme than this, the sanction of resignation is too severe. It implies that the client should have to function without proper guidance, or perhaps cease functioning at all, because its managers do not see fit to follow the advice of its advisors. If this were the consequence that should ensue from a client's refusal to follow advice, it would mean that the advice was in effect peremptory—not an informed suggestion but a command. When an advisor's advice is in effect peremptory, however, the result is a reversal of the underlying structure of responsibility for the organization's conduct. The advisor becomes the ultimate arbier and the client a subordinate. If the reversal of responsibilities becomes permanent, as it must if the advisor is deemed responsible for all critical decisions, the erstwhile advisor now becomes principal and we are back at the beginning. Furthermore, in the meantime the nominal principal has the excuse that he was merely following directions and so is not responsible for action taken in his name. Putting the point differently, when responsibility is transferred to an advisor, it is also transferred from his principal.

It seems unlikely that such a transfer of responsibility is contemplated by those who say that an advisor has some kind of responsibility for what his principal does. Probably it is assumed that the organization will not be left helpless for want of essential assistance, but rather that some other advisor will come along to take the place of the right-thinking advisor who resigns. This assumption, however, has some curious implications. It may mean that an equally high-minded advisor can step in as successor because he was not involved before. As a result, that which is reprehensible when done by one advisor in continuous service becomes acceptable when done by multiple advisors acting in a relay. A lot of moral knots are cut this way but it surely is an

Alexandrine technique. On the other hand, the assumption may be that a less high-minded successor can be expected to take over. If so, it reduces the significance of resignation to a merely personal matter and perhaps a case of narcissism. (It may also have the result of simply insulating the client from conscientious advisors in the future.) Still another possibility is that the client will figure out how to retain high-minded advisors without creating situations in which they will feel impelled to resign; the client will learn not to ask for advice in the cases that might put his counsel under that kind of pressure.

Those who insist that the ethically concerned advisor must under all circumstances act as though his client's conduct is imputable to him do not always confront the fact that a Gresham's law is at work. A client not only does not have to listen to "morally concerned" legal advice; he does not have to seek it. As long as some lawyers are willing to give whatever advice the client wants to hear, a lawyer who accepts some kind of responsibility for his client's conduct is vulnerable to being flanked. To avoid being outflanked, he has to display resiliency and to exercise some judgment about how he gives advice when a difficult matter has to be dealt with. His alternative in the real world is not to be more moral but to be amoral or unemployed.

But somewhere there is a stopping place. If it is clear that a lawyer cannot be held responsible for everything his client does, it is equally clear that he must assume responsibility at some point. The reasons he must do so are at least threefold. First, he owes a client the responsibility of putting himself on the line; at a critical juncture nothing but an implicit threat of resignation will persuade the client that the advice in question is of utmost seriousness. Second, the lawyer owes it to himself as a matter of self-respect; a lawyer with regular clients takes on their reputation, no matter what the canons say. Third, he has to maintain his reputation for professional competence. The practice of law largely involves persuading people to do things that are very unpleasant; a lawyer who cannot induce his client to do what must be done is almost certainly incapable of exercising such persuasion on others.

The way in which the lawyer assumes responsibility for the client's conduct is to give peremptory advice. Peremptory advice is in form like any other legal advice—a suggestion coupled with a supporting statement of reasons. Its tenor, however, is such that the recipient can disregard it only if he is foolish or if the advice itself is misguided.

If the advice is not misguided, it becomes peremptory because of the consequences that ensue if it is rejected. The consequences are revealed in the scenario of the "Saturday Night Massacre" involving the resignation of Elliot Richardson: The advisor resigns; the person to whom the advice was given explains the resignation to his principals; the principals then inquire into the circumstances; if the advice was misguided, the lawyer departs into oblivion; if the advice was not misguided, its recipient departs into oblivion.

Advice is made peremptory when it is cast in purely technical terms compelling a single conclusion about what to do. If the advice acknowledges that more than one course of action might be countenanced, it obviously leaves the responsibility for choice with the client. If the advice is not cast in purely technical terms—if it refers to questions of right and wrong or to "policy"—it is also not peremptory. This is because the lawyer as such has no monopoly on moral virtue or the capacity to decide questions of policy; indeed, the definition of his role at most permits him to comment on these dimensions of the matter under deliberation. A legal advisor should be reticent about incorporating morals or policy into his advice: "You can't play God"; "Who the hell are you to tell him what he ought to do?" This can be taken as indifference to questions of morals and policy. It can also be taken as an assertion that expatiation on morals and policy is not within the narrower definition of a legal advisor's domain. Hence, if the matter at hand is not of major consequence in morals or policy, the lawyer who refers to them—unless asked to do so—betrays ignorance of his auxiliary role in the decision to be made. On the other hand, if the matter at hand *is* of major consequence in morals or policy, to the point where the lawyer is prepared to assume responsibility for the decision, then the only basis on which he can do so must be technical in purport.

Advice that is technical in form and peremptory in effect can be given only under special conditions. The text of the law has to be quite clear. There has to be a substantial possibility that the law will be invoked. The consequences that may result if the law is invoked have to be serious. For a private client, this set of circumstances usually arises only when the conduct in question is what used to be called *malum in se* as distinguished from *malum prohibitum*, that is, conduct that is wrongful according to accepted morality and not simply wrong according to legal proscription. For a client who is a public official, it exists when the conduct in question would amount to an abuse of office.

The problem and the technique were well illustrated by one of the Seven Springs participants. He was speaking to the question of "unauthorized payments" by corporations—bribes. A lot can be said about whether bribes or graft payments are ever legitimate, especially if giving them is an entrenched local custom. Then, too, a legal advisor could make some kind of educational contribution to a corporate executive's business judgment by explaining that such payments might be regarded as dissipations of corporate assets, or that they could generate adverse political reaction, or that they might be dubious on moral and policy grounds. But in fact it is the law that such payments are not deductible as business expenses and that disguising them as deductions is tax fraud. Legal advice cast in these terms simply cannot be disregarded by a corporate executive. Such advice is at least as effective in guiding the company on the proper path as would be an exegesis on corporate morality; it is also consistent with the lawyer's role as legal advisor and maintains his credibility as such.

The fact that it is possible to give peremptory advice is, ultimately, the explanation of why a lawyer is responsible at some point for his client's conduct. The fact that he lawyer has to speak as advisor and not as principal explains why that point is reached only when the legal question is virtually unarguable. In the end, the boundary between a preposition that is legally arguable and one that is not pretty well conforms to the boundary between fundamental right and wrong in everyday life, wherever that is. A good lawyer has to know where it is. A lawyer who does not know where it is also does not know when to keep open the client's options and when to close them, and therefore how to give good advice when it is most needed.

11. Concluding Reflections

The central ideas in the legal profession's code of ethics originally arose out of criminal cases, particularly the defense of criminal cases. It is an historical fact that two criminal cases were the first occasions on which a lawyer's ethics were searchingly considered. One was Lord Brougham's representation of Queen Caroline concerning a charge of adultery that her husband, George IV, contemplated levying against her. In discussing the matter, with the aim of forestalling a prosecution, Brougham stated that he considered protection of the client was the advocate's

> first and only duty; and in performing this duty he ... must go on reckless of the consequences, though it should be his unhappy fate to involve his country in confusion.

The other case was a prosectuion for murder of a man whom his counsel discovered, during trial, was in fact guilty. Counsel nevertheless played out the defense, putting a key prosecution witness through a gruelling and suggestive cross-examination. The ensuing professional debate concerning his conduct established the principle that an advocate is responsible only for presenting the best possible case for his client and not for the truth.[1]

The courses of action of counsel in both these cases in retrospect still appear to have been right. The principles

---

1. See Mellinkoff, *The Conscience of a Lawyer* (1973), for an account.

CONCLUDING REFLECTIONS

argued in support of their conduct may also still be right as applied to an advocate in defending the prosecution of a serious criminal offense. But these instances and these principles have been extended as the foundation of the rules of ethics that govern the legal profession in rendering other services in other contexts. This transposition of analysis cannot be sound, any more than it would be sound to say that the privilege against self-incrimination should be the standard of disclosure that operates in the marketplace and the boardroom and the normal administration of the income tax laws. The ethical foundation sustaining the narrow function of the criminal defense lawyer simply cannot carry the system of ethics for the whole range of function that American lawyers now perform.

One wonders whether the criminal defense model is retained because it results in maximum immunity from responsibility. The tenor of the bar's Code would suggest this. The Code conveys the impression that, except in relations with other lawyers, a lawyer is never in the picture of what his client may do. He simply finds loopholes or acts as a mouthpiece, just as folks have always said.

If this is the bar's portrayal of the lawyer's role, it is not an attractive one. It certainly does not resemble the self-image of other professionals. Certified public accountants, for example, see themselves as being judges of their clients and not merely their advocates. Doctors if anything err on the other side, assuming to make decisions for their patients that many observers think should at least be shared by the patient, through the mechanism of "informed consent." And the portrait of the lawyer as merely a technical adviser and spokesperson is false. The fact is that the modern legal adviser is an actor in the situations in which he gives advice. And as such he is accountable.

Perhaps lawyers hang on to the old claim of immunity because they cannot see an acceptable alternative. Once it is said that a lawyer is responsible for some of what his client does, there does not seem to be any stopping place that can be clearly described in a rule. But of course rules can be devised to deal with open-ended problems, as they have been in the rules lawyers write for others. The technique is to say that one should act as "a reasonable person" would act in the circumstances. This is the standard that applies to doctors, accountants, trustees, manufacturers, and motorists. A rule of that kind does not give definite guidance, but that is a peril that can be lived with. If lawyers are waiting for a more definitive rule they should know better. Certainly the absence of certitude is no justification for lawyers refusing to accept their moral involvement in the matters in which they act and advise.

One more word. Why should good lawyers represent big corporations, instead of the poor and the oppressed? Not an easy question to answer, but something can be said to it. In the first place, it is not clearly a fact that the good lawyers—meaning in this connection those having high technical proficiency—do represent only the big corporations. While in general the bar most highly esteems the lawyers who specialize in antitrust, securities, and tax work, it does not follow that this is a fair estimate of the relative difficulty of these specialities compared with others. But weight has to be given to this professional estimate, and taking it into account leads to another point.

One of the chief reasons why competent lawyers go into corporate work is precisely that business clients are willing to invest enough in their lawyers to permit them to develop the highest possible levels of professional skill. Indeed, it is not far wrong to say that lawyers for big corporations are the only practitioners regularly afforded latitude to give their technical best to the problems they work on. The rest of the bar ordinarily has to slop through with quickie work or, as one lawyer put it, make good guesses as to the level of malpractice at which they should operate in any given situation. If practicing ethically includes performing with all the care and thoroughness that one is capable of, practice on behalf of the big corporations may be the most ethical kind. At any rate, critics of corporation lawyers might also notice that the most proficient doctors are at the big hospitals and not the county health services, that the most proficient journalists are with the national media and not the Utica *Tribune*, and that leading sociologists do not teach in junior college.

Then, of course, there is the money.

Appendix

Seven Springs Center Symposium
The Ethical Lawyer and His Client
June 17-19 and July 15-17, 1976

Oscar M. Ruebhausen, Chairman	Debevoise, Plimpton, Lyons & Gates
Joseph N. Greene, Jr.**	President, Seven Springs Center
Geoffrey C. Hazard, Jr.	Professor, Yale Law School; Seven Springs Associate for Legal Studies
Margaret Mason	Student, Yale Law School
Steven Champlin	Student, Yale Divinity School
Thomas Divine	Student, Yale Law School

Membership of the Symposium

George W. Coombe, Jr.	Executive Vice President and General Counsel, Bank of America
Lloyd N. Cutler*	Wilmer, Cutler & Pickering
John Doar**	Donovan, Leisure, Newton & Irvine
Donald J. Evans*	Goodwin, Procter & Hoar
James Fishkin	Assistant Professor of Political Science, Yale University
Judge Marvin E. Frankel*	United States District Court, New York

*Attended June session only.
**Attended July session only.

APPENDIX

George C. Freeman, Jr.	Hunton, Williams & Gay
Grenville Garside**	Staff Director and Special Counsel, Senate Committee on Interior and Insular Affairs
Herbert J. Hansell	Jones, Day, Reavis & Pogue
Everett L. Hollis	Mayer, Brown & Platt
Robert Kasanof*	Baer & McGoldrick
William F. Kennedy	General Counsel, General Electric Company
Leon S. Lipson*	Professor of Law, Yale University
William Pincus**	President, Council on Legal Education for Professional Responsibility, Inc.
Nelson W. Polsby**	Professor of Political Science, University of California at Berkeley
Ronald D. Rotunda	Professor of Law, University of Illinois at Urbana-Champaign
Antonin Scalia**	Assistant Attorney General, Office of Legal Counsel, U.S. Department of Justice
Orville H. Schell*	Hughes, Hubbard & Reed
Murray L. Schwartz**	Professor of Law, University of California at Los Angeles
David Sills*	Social Science Research Council
Peter O. A. Solbert	Davis, Polk & Wardwell
Thomas S. Tresselt**	Assistant Dean, Yale Law School
Stanton Wheeler**	Professor of Law and Sociology, Yale University
Frank Wozencraft*	Baker & Botts
Robert V. Zener**	Deputy General Counsel, Environmental Protection Agency

Index

Adams, John, 122
Adversary system, 120–35
Advertising, 106
Advisory opinions of bar associations, 59–60
American Bar Association: Canons of Professional Ethics of, 18–19, 26; Code of Professional Responsibility of, *see* Code of Professional Responsibility; Committee on Professional Ethics of, 42
Arbitration, 124
Arnold, Thurman, 86
Attorney-client privilege: definition of, 22–23; fraud under, 39; principle of loyalty in, 33

Bar associations: advisory opinions on ethics by, 59–60; fee schedules of, 98; political activities of, 93
Bargaining: conflict of interest in, 73–86; cost in, 74
Boston Massacre, 122
Brandeis, Louis D., 58–59, 60–61, 62, 64, 65, 92
Brougham, Lord, 150
Brownell, Herbert, 111
Burke, Edmund, 1

"Canons" (Code of Professional Responsibility), 6
Canons of Professional Ethics, 18–19, 26
Caroline (queen of England), 150
Charity in legal service, 88–89
Chicago Seven trial, 134

Civil disobedience, 10–11
Civil rights movement, 92
Civil Service (Great Britain), 118
Clients: in adversary system, 122, 129–30; attorney-client privilege and, *see* Attorney-client privilege; Code of Professional Responsibility on, 8–9; confidentiality and, 20–33; government agencies as, 54–56, identification of, 43–45; large organizations as, 46–54; legal assistance to poor and, 88–89; nonclient responsibilities of lawyers and, 45–46; professional ethics and, 3; refusal to follow lawyers' advice by, 136–49; responsibility of lawyer for actions of, 144–48; unpopular clients and, 87–96
Code of Professional Responsibility: "Canons" of, 6; civil disobedience under, 10–11; client frauds and crimes disclosure under, 25–27; client identification under, 45; confidentiality under, 20–33; conflict of interest under, 8, 20, 21, 33–38; constituency of lawyers treated in, 8–9; criminal defense model in, 151; Disciplinary Rules of, 6–7, 19; "Ethical Considerations" of, 6; ethical statements in, 6–11; fees under, 97–98; full disclosure under, 9–10; history of, 18–19; lawyer for the situation and, 62–63; lawyers' attitudes toward, 6–7; legal advisor's role in, 137–38, 139;

INDEX

principle of loyalty statement in, 33; prohibited assistance under, 20, 21, 38–42
Committee on Professional Ethics, 42
Competition: and fees, 100
Confidentiality: attorney-client privilege and, 22–23; client fraud and crimes disclosure under, 25–27; Code of Professional Responsibility on, 20–33; corporations and, 50–53, 55–56; disclosure-with-consent rule in, 24–25; distinction between past and future under, 27–31; embarrassing or detrimental information under, 22, 23–24; government agencies as clients and, 55–56; identification of clients and, 31; third-party wrongdoing under, 31–32; types of matters under, 21–22
Conflict of interest, 69–86; bargaining and, 73–86; business transactions exception to, 33–34; Code of Professional Responsibility on, 8, 20, 21, 33–38; culture of law and, 79–80; large law firms and, 81–83; lawyer for the situation and, 60; litigation and, 70–73; payment by third party and, 34–35; positional conflicts in large law firms and, 90–92; principle of loyalty in, 33; professional judgment of lawyers in, 76–78, 84; prohibited assistance and, 84–85; representation of clients with conflicting interests, 35–38; revolving door practice and, 108, 116
Congress, 54, 117, 118
Corporations: adversary system and, 132–33; client identification in, 43, 46–54; conflict of interest in services to, 69–70, 72, 80; cost of legal services to, 103–04; general counsel in, 141–44; law departments in, 103–04, 105–06; lawyer for the situation and, 62; legal advice sought by, 140–41; legal conception of, 47–48; positional conflicts in law firms and, 91, 94–95; reasons for lawyers representing, 152–53; rule of confidentiality and, 50–53, 55–56; use of bribes by, 148–49
Courts: and fee questions, 98

Dean, John, 84
Disciplinary proceedings, 59
Disciplinary Rules (Code of Professional Responsibility), 6–7, 19
Disclosure-with-consent rule, 24–25
Disqualification rule, 109–13
Due process, 122

Ehrlichman, John, 71
Eisenhower, Dwight D., 111
English law, 89, 118, 120–21, 122, 131
"Ethical Considerations" (Code of Professional Responsibility), 6
Evidence: adversary system and, 121, 122, 123, 126; prohibited assistance on, 39

Federal Legal Services Program, 88, 92–93
Fees, 97–106; adversary system and, 131, 134; client's refusal of advice and, 139; Code of Professional Responsibility on, 97–98; competition and, 100; conflict of interest and, 34–35; corporate clients and, 103–04; division of, 98–99; in English system, 131; to government agencies, 104–05; law office management and,

INDEX

Fees *(continued)* 100–01; lawyers' compensation in, 101–02; personal injury litigation and, 132; referral fees and, 98–99
France, 120
Frankel, Judge Marvin, 123
Fraud: bargaining and, 74; disclosure of, 25–27; prohibited assistance and, 39, 40
Full disclosure: Code of Professional Responsibility on, 9–10; conflict of interest and, 36, 76

General counsel: in corporations, 141–44
George IV (king of England), 150
Germany, 120
Government agencies: alternative model of service in, 114–17; bargaining in, 73; client identification in, 43, 46, 54–56; cost of legal services to, 104–05; lawyer for the situation and, 62; legal review in, 80; patronage system in, 108, 117; regulation of professions by, 16–18; revolving door practice in, 107–19; rule of confidentiality and, 55–56
Great Britain, 89, 118, 120–21, 122
Gulf Oil Corporation, 141

Haldeman, John, 71
Hamilton, Andrew, 122
Hand, Judge Learned, 1, 135

Jackson, Andrew, 117
Japan, 80
Judges: in adversary system, 120, 124
Jury system, 120, 124–25

Law departments, corporate, 103–06

Law firms: conflict of interest in, 81–83, 90–96; revolving door practice and, 111–12
Law office management, 100–01
Lawyer for the situation, 58–68; Code of Professional Responsibility on, 62–63; cost and, 74; defining role in, 65–68; origin of term, 58–59
Legal aid services, 88

McCloy, John, 141
Management in law offices, 100–01
Miranda warnings, 50–52
Mitchell, John, 84

Nader, Ralph, 118
Nixon, Richard M., 35

Patronage system, 108, 117
Perjury, 129, 130
Personal injury litigation, 91, 98–99, 132
Poor: and legal assistance, 88–89
Prohibited assistance: Code of Professional Responsibility on, 20, 21, 38–42; conflict of interest and, 84–85
Prosecutors: in adversary system, 125, 126

Race discrimination cases, 92, 94
Referral fees, 98–99
Revolving door practice, 107–19; alternative model for, 114–17; concept of "a matter" in, 110; disqualification rule in, 109–13; legal controls in, 109–10; principle of imputation in, 110–11
Richardson, Elliot, 147

St. Clair, James, 35
Sandburg, Carl, 1
Scottsboro case, 122

INDEX

Shakespeare, William, 1
Sharswood, Judge George, 18–19
Shaw, George Bernard, 132
Small claims court, 122
Socialist countries, 125–26
Soviet Union, 125
Supreme Court, 98, 106, 122

Trials: and adversary system, 120–35
Tweed, Harrison, 93

Watergate, 54, 71, 84, 85, 105
Wilson, Woodrow, 58

Yugoslavia, 126

Zenger, John Peter, 122

KF
306
.H3
1978

Hazard, Geoffrey C.
    Ethics in the practice
of law